"Have sextant, will travel"

Pioneers or Guinea Pigs?

By

Andy Kelly

ISBN: 1-4033-2107-8 (e-book)
ISBN: 1-4033-2108-6 (Paperback)
ISBN: 1-4033-6472-9 (Hardcover)

Library of Congress Control Number: 2002093979

This book is printed on acid free paper.

Printed in the United States of America
Bloomington, IN

1stBooks - rev. 10/01/02

Contents

Andy Kelly i

Have Sextant will travel. 1

Pioneers or Guinea Pigs. 142

(Celestial Navigation has been replaced by

Global Positioning)

Captain Evans defined. 166

Have Sextant will travel.

As a teenager and an unemployed drop out living on the wrong side of the tracks during our nation's worst depression,, what would be the odds of surviving that depression, of traveling to four corners of the globe, of meeting world figures, military and business, of becoming successful in both the military and business worlds?

Yes, those odds were staggering, yet, at the time, those possibilities were the furthest from my mine., as the biggest worry then was what, would we have to eat that day?

My mother, (a recent widow) with eight children was surviving the very recent loss of her husband and a 19 year old daughter, (Kathryn Veronica) was facing, almost unsurmountable odds.

She, with no income, no way to pay the mortgage, no funds to feed the remaining 8 children, face a gigantic task of survival.

At that time, there were no public assistance programs to assist families like ours, and if there were her strong Irish pride would not have allowed her to accept them. The only food on the table was earned by odd jobs that we, the six boys and or the 2 girls might find. Our 2 youngest boys, later became victims of malnutrition, but we all did manage to survive.

I, a high school dropout was adrift until my brother Jim, a member of the Pennsylvania National Guard, took me to one of his meetings. I was very impressed and joined the 176th Field Artillery Battalian of the 29th Division of the Pennsylvania National guard, in the late summer of 1939. That was the turning point of my life when the luck started to run in my direction and remained there for the rest of my life. A friend of mine, Wally Schmitt, also joined with me and we found the program and the opportunities to do some thing practical most interesting. The Guard members went out of their way to make us feel welcome and we really enjoyed meeting so many of those sergeants, corporals and the privates who seemed like they actually wanted us to be members of their military family.

As their annual active duty tour for the year had just been completed, we would have to wait til next summer when they would be encamping at A.P.Hill in Virginia.

We were a field artillery unit utilizing both 75 and 155 milimeter howitzers and when we got to A.P.Hill we found it was comprised of a large tent area, with 4 men to a tent, an out door mess tent and out door latrines. For city boys it really it was really a different style of living that wood take a little time getting used to, but the but the more we did the more we liked it.

We were introduced to M-1 rifles, machine guns, two types of howitzers and 45 calibre pistols. Naturally, in just two weeks we did not become experts on any of them.We did find the meaning of teamwork, especially with those howitzers. A crew of four privates, plus a corporal, were assigned different duties in coupling the guns to a weapons carrier, tow it to a gun sight, uncouple it and set it up to fire, place a number of missiles near it, to load it, but dry fire only, quickly break it back down, rehook it to the truck again and return to our area.

Those two weeks fled by and we, reluctantly, returned to Pittsburgh and the one night a month meetings. However at this time a certain Mr. Hitler was warming up in Europe by running rampantly over Poland and other small nations.

This created my rumors that we would soon become Federalized and be sent to a nearby military base.

In fact a number of other States Guard Units were being activated in the fall of 1940 and sent to some of those permanent Forts.

We were notified in December, that in early January we'd be Federalized and sent to Fort Meade, Maryland. This proved to be true and we went by train to Fort Meade, to become a "training cadre" for "selectees" who were now being "drafted".. We were told they were to be addressed as "selectees".

As we were not very well versed in anything,as yet, to be training others we were being "force fed" in every area we were to instruct them in. The area we were in was not as yet even being close to finished, so we lived in tents, in about 10 degree weather. We had only mud roads and a few barracks about one fourth completed. They would house 100 men, but in the mean time we slept and ate in tents, We had 4 men to a tent and had to really keep moving around to stay warm.

Our Commander, a Captain Harold A. Evans,was a real task master and a strong advocate of clean tents and later clean barracks we finally were able to move in, as well as a strict dress code. We each had a cot with a footlocker at the end of it. The shoes had to be lined up in a set pattern and they better be shining like a reflector. The beds had to be so taut that you could bounce a quarter of them and they had to have "hospital" corners.

He was the same with weapons, trucks, (mostly weapon's carriers as well as with marching. For no matter what the occasion, his battery would be not (and was) in the "whole damned" division.

Our barracks were spotless and every Friday night was cleaning night and the barracks were scrubbed down. On Saturday morning he had a "White Glove" inspection and if we didn't pass it there were no passes for the week end issued. We soon earned the nickname of "The Old Ladies Home" but we were the cleanest in "The whole Damned Division".

In marching drills whether, on the road or in the fields we had to march "at attention" as any one can do it on the parade grounds, but we would do it every where. He really wasn't a martinet as there was nothing he would make us do that he couldn't do and do it better. I never realized how how strict he was until I was later in Aviation Cadet School and did not pick up a single demerit, while all the other cadets picked them up almost daily.

In early April our "selectees" began to arrive to find that Captain Evans had made us quite competent instructors in about every phase: manning howitzers, driving vehicles, firing machine guns. M-1 rifles and 45 calibre pistols, and we soon made many new friends among those "selectees".

When we first arrived at Fort Meade in January I was a PFC)private first class). But when the selectees arrived and our numbers increase, I was made a Corporal. As I said Mr. Hitlers was taking over almost all of Europe via his "blitzkreig" or "lightning war" with those special unstoppable tanks tanks.

This caused the Pentagon to try new types of weaponry one of which was to be known as "a Tank Destroyer Battalian and would be a variation of the howitzers now in use, they were 75 and 155 milimeter howitzers which lobbed their shells for long distances. But now they would need them (the shells) for direct firing at close range, this would necessitate using smaller shells: 55 mm and new 37 mm at close range at those tanks. To get this new new venture off ground they would take the nucleus of those units from the existing field artillery units., starting with us.

I was part of the initially picked cadres to form such a unit and we were to become the very first ":Tank Destroyer Battalians as the 639th Tank Destroyer Battalian. I went from Corporal to Buck sergeant (3 stripes) to platoon (staff) sergeant- (3 stripes with a rocker) in a month.

Author as a platoon sergeant in his barracks room studying.

When the new 37 mm direct fire guns arrrived I was given: six weapons carrires, four guns, two buck sergeants, four corporals and eight privates to form into my platoon, with each gun being manned by two privates and one corporal. Each sergeant had two gun crews to head up.

We had regular sessions of hooking up the guns to the weapons carriers towing to an area, the unhooking from the weapons carriers, settting the guns into firing positions, arranging the shells for easy accessibility. Speed had to be the main criteria, as anti tank weapons to to be speedily driven to an area nearby moving tanks, set up rapidly, fire and get the h--- out of there in a hurry as Hitler's tanks were very mobile and you would not have much time to set up and fire at them.

The army scheduled extensive maneuvers all over the south to last for 3 to 4 months. Our outfit, the 639th Tank Destroyer Bn. went with the 29th Division and once again we were in tent cities only this time in an area loaded with rattle snakes, copper heads and coral snakes, all very poisonous. Needless to say you constantly checked every thing, especially your bed roll every night.

. Many times we were the Blue Army combatting the Red Army in both North and South Carolina. In those maneuvers we slept out doors but I always slept in the back of my weapons carrier. I found that many of our selectees were from Virginia and had little or no fear of snakes and readily slept on the ground.

There were many black snakes (non poisonous) and when those selectees found any they just threw them into the many bonfires. We had a Major Johnson who wore those short military boots that only went partly up on his calves and he had the habit of stomping on those copper heads. I often wondered why the snakes weren't able to bite him above those small boots.

Those maneuvers were extensive and we were still very actively involved when the Japs struck Pearl Harbor. No one knew where Pearl Harbor was, or why a little punk nation like Japan attack us, why it couldn't possibly last over 2 or 3 months.

We were immediately ordered back to our home bases to await further orders. When we arrived at Fort Meade there were myriads of programs seeking volunteers for new types of duties. One that interested me was the "Flying

Sergeants" that was expanding, as they were all staff Sergeant pilots, as that was my rank.

How ever the sergeant, at Division H.Q. said I was 3 months too old, but there was a new Aviation Cadet Program on the way to him and to call him back in a few days, but I also applied for the infantry officer program.

In a few days I was informed that new aviation cadet program was now open for volunteers to take a special very detailed test, called the Minnesota Multiphasic program. It was and 8 hour test in which there were word associations, mathematics, english word associations, putting square pegs into round holes and other little gimmicks.

The program had one item that really bothered me in that it said you had to have a minimum of 2 years of college to qualify for it.Although I only had 2 years of high school. I said on my my application that I had 2 years of college.

One hundred and twenty of us took the tests. Several days later I was notified that only twelve had passed it, and I was one of the twelve. Then we were subjected to personal interviews to see if we measured up to what they were looking for. and, believe it or not, I was one of the six who were accepted. We were then given thirty day furloughs (furloughs for enlisted and leaves for officers), so I departed for Pittsburgh immediately.

While I was home the entire 29th Division packed up and headed for Europe.They hit the beaches in France while I was home.

I forgot to mention that I was scheduled for an interview for Infantry Officer School at one o'clock the same day I was summoned to the main post for the results of the Aviation Cadet interviews and was notified that I was one of those accepted. Needless to say I immediately cancelled that interview. I dread to think what could have happened if those interviews had been reversed.

While I was at home I received a wire extending my furlough for thirty more days and when I returned to the mainpost (my old outfit had been shipped out) the sergeant asked "how much money do you have on you".

When I asked "why"? He said "Those schools still aren't ready, so go home for ten more days"

The reason for those extended aviation cadet programs was that the war in Europe and far East demanded many more supplies, men, etc. and there were too few planes to get the school cadres to the schools and were needed. `Now multiphasic tests merely qualified to apply to those schools, but to no one in particular. So we were sent to a school at Selman Field in Alabama for testing to determine which categories we were most suited for.

So after extensive interviews and quizzes I was sent to Maxwell Field, also in Alabama for a nine week course in thirty different subjects to get used to schooling again. How ever you must pass every subject with a minimum grade of eighty percent in each.

Upon completion, I was informed that I, as one of the top level students, qualified for navigation training and would be assigned to the Pan American Air Ways School at the

University of Miami, Fla. We, of the navigator selectees, felt quite elated that the top ones would be navigators but later learned that the top ones were picked for what was needed the most "at the time", be it pilot, bombardier or a navigator.

Upon completion of those nine weeks we were given thirty five days delay in "enroute" to Coral Gables, Fla. that was less than three hundred miles away??

`But it was they were not ready for us which resulted in such a long delay. But again it was a very lucky break for me to have over thirty days at home as my sister was a Nun teaching at the Sisters of Charity Order of Elizabeth Seton School for Girls in Pittsburgh. The school was a former public grade school about ten blocks from where I grew up and when the school district built a new school the Nuns bought the old one.

When I asked her if I could get some brushing up on "math" she arranged for a Nun to teach me advanced math for a month:

geometry, algebra, trigonometry. etc all day long for five days a week for a month.

Another break came my way in that the Buhl Planetarium in Pittsburgh was having nightly sessions on astronomy as well as star identification classes. So I was able to sign up for them as did my youngest brother who was home on vacation from Notre Dame University.

As I had only completed two years of high school, I needed all of the mathematics and star identification help that I could get, as that would allow me to focus on other subjects while my class mates would be focussing on both mathematics and star identification. With out the help on both I would have had a very rough time in cadet school. Now Pan Am Air Ways had a most unique history for, as I had said, the Army Air Corps (not yet Air Force) had few navigators and none of them were accomplished in Celestial navigation or qualified to fly long distances over water.

It was in 1939 that a General Emmons (from the Pentagon) was on a flight to Europe on one of Pan Am Clipper ships. Pan Am was the only major carrier to fly the oceans. They recruited navigators from surface ships who had a limited knowledged in celestial navigation and they trained them, via their methods, to become aerial celestial navigators in their flying boats.

The navigator on General Emmons flight, was named Charley Lunn and as they were approaching the Azores, on the route to Spain, the General was standing by Lunn's desk when they passed over the small island of Horta, in the Azores chain. They flew over the island on Mr. Lunn' eta and right on course.

General Emmons said, "I'll bet you feel pretty good that you hit that little island right on the button".. To which Mr. Lunn said "No sir, I would have been disappointed if I hadn't".

The General was quite impressed and asked him "How many navigators could you teach to become navigators"? To which he replied, "Why to as many as could hear my voice". That was in 1937 and though the idea of the school was discussed and Charley Lunn agreed to head it up, when and if it could be arranged. But it wasn't actually opened til mid 1940 at the University of Miami, Fla. So the following is my recollection of how I was able to hire out my sextant.

The title "Have sextant Will Travel, was inspired by the famous Richard Boone's "Have Gun Will Travel" television series.

Though he made his living via his gun and traveled the old west to ply his trade. We similarly hired out "our sextants" but we traveled the world to ply our trade.

Even before the U.S. became involved in WW-11, while England was waging an almost losing battle with Hitler, we were supplying them with much needed materials, planes and equipment. Many of our plants worked extra shifts manufacturing those needed items, but the attack at Pearl Harbor created even greater demand upon our plants to produce and the our military to deliver; more aircraft: bombers, cargo, fighters. Plus accellerate training of aircrews: pilots, navigators,bombardiers, radio operators and crew chiefs..

A serious drawback was that the type of navigators they were training for the Army Air Corps were for short or medium range missions, mostly overland. Too little emphacis had been placed on training the navigation students in the art of celestial or loran navigational methods. Nor were our planes equipped with necessary instruments to utilize either which added to the problems of delivering that much needed material, via air, to the various theatres: near or far East, to Europe, Africa and the south Pacific, that would involve long stretches of over water flying with navigators skilled in both celestial and loran systems of navigation of which there were none at the time.

Loran was short for "long range aerial navigation" that was designed especially for over water flying. It entailed the use of radio signals (that incidently were not suited for overland flying as the earth absorbed the signals that eminated from a "master station to send a signal to a slave station" that then sent it to both the aircraft and back to the master station.

Pan American Airways, til then, was the only transoceanic airline (operating out of the USA to foreign shores via huge flying boats or "Clippers" as they were so known.

They specialized in celestial navigation as 90% of their flying was over water, at night time when the stars were visible, whereas in daylight only the sun is visible which provided a single "line of position", or a great circle completely around the earth. That one "LOP" positioned you on it but "not specifically where" so you needed at least two lines that crossed each other to locate yourself.

With aircraft in around the clock production, and accellerated crew training, there was more need to train special navigators capable of guiding the planes and crews to any point on earth, especially over water..

The Army Air Corps (name at that time) contracted with Charlie Lunn, then head navigator of Pan Am, to establish a training facility for specially selected cadets in very specialized courses of celestial navigation in conjunction with the traditional methods: map reading, dead reckoning, and radio.

The program became so universally accepted that all of our allied nations requested permission to have members of their crews admitted to the training. We had Chiang Kai Chek's nephew (Peter Chu) in our class as well as military from south America, England, France, Australia, Canada and nations around the globe.

We trained in those old German flying boats, twin engine Condors that indicated only 75 knots per hour. A nautical mile is 1.15 statute miles so we were indicating less than 100 miles an hour. (more on this later).

We used the hand held A-12 sextants with which you "shot" the sun and moon via the eye glass but as stars were dimmer we had to "shoot" them via it's reflective glass.

Due to the varied motions of all aircraft: (yew, haw & roll) forward, backward, sidewards, with slight rolls thrown in, it was found that in order to compensate for those motions we would have to "shoot" each body for exactly two minutes while clicking the trigger arrangement that made horizontal markings on the sextant wheel. We then had to visually determine the center of all of those markings as our "observed altitude" or the "midpoint" of the shooting.

It was a tricky maneuver as the sextant contained a small flat, circular container that was about a quarter inch in thickness and was about one and a half inches in diameter. It contained two circular lenses enclosed in a metal band with a liquid sealed inside it containing a small air bubble that floated in that liquid.

When "shooting" any celestial body: star, moon, sun, or planet, that bubble had to be exactly in the center of that tiny chamber and the body "being shot" exactly in the dead center of the bubble.

This required much practice and concentration to accomplish it, taking weeks to do so but, strangely, after you did it so often it soon became so natural that you unconsciouly did it every time. Your mind and eye co-ordinated instantly and it would have taken a conscious effort to keep it out of the center, even while the plane was being buffetted by winds and clouds.

"Observed altitude" was obtained by "shooting" any celestial body for exactly a two minute time frame.Those "Shot's" mid point was measured in "Greenwich time" and checked against the almanac containing the "true positions" of <u>every navigable body of every area</u> <u>of the globe</u> as declination and sidereal hour angle corresponding to earth's latitude and longitude. This gave a "line of position or a great circle that travelled completely around the earth. Your aircraft was on that line but, exactly where you could not ascertain until you shot one or more"lines of position that crossed each other preferably three of them in the shape of a triangle.

You compared those "observed altitudes" with the true altitudes listed in the manual at the exact same second as your mid-point. The manual gave you the body's exact heighth and azimuth of it's specific area above the earth at that exact second placing you on it's great circle but where, you couldn't know until you plotted several form your triangle.

You had to shoot three bodies, if available, hopefully one exactly dead ahead, or directly behind the plane to serve as a speed line. But first you shot one either forty five degrees to right of your heading, called a course line) then your speed line and finally one at three hundred fifteen degrees to your left (another course line) or as close to those angles as possible.

First you shot a course line, plotted it, shot a speed line and plotted it and finally your last course line and plotted it. Your speed line gave you a positive position between your last "fix" so you could measure your ground speed. Using that ground speed you moved the first course line back to and the second course line up to your speed line, and if you had made some good "shots" you had a very tight triangle and knew "exactly where you were".

This enabled you to compute the exact "track" you were making and then you could plot your exact ground speed against your indicated air speed, check your exact drift (right or left of course) to determine wind direction and speed.

You then radio'd your position, wind direction and speed & cloud patterns (at your altitude) to either the departure area or to your destination for their files (every half hour) which other crews flying in that area would use to plot their courses.

The way you determined those wind speeds and direction was via a hand held "E-6-B" computor that was your right arm in determining drifts and ground speeds, in conjunction with the drift meter that you used to measure the white caps for both ground speed and drift in the day time, when weather permitted.

When possible we used Loran, which worked as I said with a master station on shore, a slave station (usually a ship at sea that traveled in a 3 mile radius not straying from it's assigned area). The slave station received the signal from the master station and continued it on to us to give us a single line of position, also a great circle. We then used a second Loran station for a second "lop" and where they crossed it exactly where you were and it only took about two minutes.

But the disadvantage of Loran was that it could not be used over land and it did not completey span the oceans. It depended upon the master stations on shore and the slave stations several hundred miles off the coast making it very limited in it's usage.

As I said Loran was merely a radio signal whose pulse was measured from the time it left the master station, went to the slave station, to the aircraft and back to the master station. It was a great asset,when available, but the original sets had 22 screw driver adjustments, which we learned to use. However so many dunces thought they could also do it you mainly found the unit "out of sync" and it would take you about 45 minutes to reset it.

But back to school, upon graduation day (Dec. 12- 1942) we were commissioned as 2nd. lieutenants and given the wings of a navigator (along with the appellation of "Magellan"). We were given ten days "leaves" (as we were now officers and it was no longer called a furlough) of ten days before reporting for transitional training in medium bombers and transport planes, mostly B-25's.

After training on those old Condors at 100 miles per hour at about 5,000 feet and reading those white caps in the drift meter so easily and then suddenly flying in those B-25's at over 250 mph at 200 foot altitudes you couldn't read drift, as everything went by so fast. But eventually as in learning how to use those sextants, you also became accustomed to using the drift meter at those low altitudes and the higher speeds.

During that transitional period we were housed at the Roubideau Hotel in St. Joseph, Missouri as the air base had no room to house us.

A most interesting occurrence happened to us during our stay there. We found the gathering place for the local girls at the Katz Drug Store in down town "St. Joe" as the locals referred to it. The drug store had a large ice cream bar as well as a sandwich bar where you could spend time over a soda or cup of coffee and a sandwich. We would, mostly in pairs stop in for a sandwich or a soft drink. After about a half hour we would return to the hotel.

Soon after returning to our rooms we would begin to get phone calls and the caller was a young girl, in her late teens or early twenties. They ask for us by name and each would say, "Why didn't call me when you got back into town "?

Now we had never been there before and the caller would say, "why didn't you come back down town or to my home "? She'd say "don't you remember me"? Then they gave you their name and phone number.

The way they knew our names was that we were all wearing our new A-2 jackets, upon which our names printed upon them. Now to make a long story short, they all knew that we had never been there before, as well as that we were all brand new "shavetails" the name for new second Lieutenants and each with ten thousand dollars of life insurance and they were doing their very best to marry as many of them they could. Some were married to four and five new officers who would soon be going into combat and many would not be coming home.

As each officer had a different name and if they died their life insurance would go to a different last name with very little chance of them being caught. If one or more was not killed he would come home and live with her, unless she moved.

We called it "Shave Tail Roulette" but it evidently did work. In fact I met some of them who came to the duty station with her new husband. Of course we never told the guy that he had been suckered.

After several weeks of transition we were shipped to the 552nd AAF Base Unit of the

2nd. Ferry Group at the New Castle Air Base in Wilmingon, Del., and assigned to the 8th transport squadron.

This would merely be our headquarters as the squadron would "hire us out" to any base needing navigators to take their planes and crews overseas. We would replace the navigators of the planes assigned crews but only until we had delivered the plane to it's duty station be it: England, Africa, India, China,, Italy, etc. And then find our ways home again. The dumb part of it was that the planes regular navigator was usually shipped via boat to his destination, instead of leaving him ride along for the experience.

When I delivered 7 A-20 medium bombers to Italy, (in mid 44), all of the crews navigators were shipped via surface transportion while their stations on board the A-20's were vacant.

My first mission was to augment the crew of a C-87 (a cargo version of the B-24) just out of the factory and to take it to Chabua, India. It was the start of my career that paralled the radio show "Have gun will travel", except I carried a sextant instead of a gun.

At the time I hadn't the slightest idea that our special expertise would result in so many trips to (almost exotic) foreign lands, meet so many world leaders, dignitaries top military and government officials, foreign diplomats, war heroes, dedicated flight nurses and have varied experiences that even the most vivid imagination couldn't have predicted.

That first assignment took that fully loaded C-87 to Chabua, India via the south Atlantic route: Puerto Rica, Trinidad, Guyana, Brazil, Africa, Egypt, Arabia and on into 3 areas of India: Kurachi, New Delhi and finally Assam, on the border of Burma.

Can you imagine the thoughts running through the mind of this young kid (from the other side of the tracks in Pittsburgh, Pa). taking an expensive four engined aircraft, loaded with valuable cargo, 19 passengers and a crew of 5 half way around the world to a spot none of us had ever even heard of until we read our orders. I was to guide that plane, as I said, more than 12,000 miles over the Atlantic Ocean, the jungles of central and south America, over Africa, the deserts, the mediterranean sea, Arabia, transverse the wide expanse of India to a little airstrip in the province of Assam on the border of Burma.

Scared? You bet your boots I was, going to areas you had only seen in news reels (no t.v. in those days) or in magazines. Til then the most responsibility I had been given was my anti-tank platoon in the 176th Field artillery at Ft. Meade, Md., when I was a platoon sergeant with four 37 mm anti-tank guns, six weapons loader vehicles and a squad of buck sergeant, 4 corporals and and 8 privates, now I would have to be responsible for an expensive plane, it's cargo and 25 men (passengers and crew).

We picked up the C-87 at the factory in Minneapolis, flew to Memphis, Tenn., where we loaded the cargo, passengers and departed for Morrison Field in West Palm Beach, Fla.,then headed for Chabua, India via Puerto Rico and points south.

In Puerto Rico we saw our first Bob Hope show, with Jerry Colonna and many movie starlets. We were also introduced to the British shirt and shorts outfit that everyone was wearing. Their short sleeves were a little longer than ours as were the shorts that hung lower than ours. They sure didn't enhance the arms and legs of a six foot, one inch tall skinny navigator.

Once we left the shores of the USA dress codes went out the window and the only immediate authority was the plane's commander, Captain Ackerman (from Gunther, Alabama) and he made no comment when we climbed aboard in that regalia and headed out for Port Au Spain, in Trinidad.

We R.O.N.'ed there and were about to take off for Waller Field, in British Guyana, when a P-39 going past our taxi strip accidently chewed off our right wing tip. Although we had fuel tanks in the wings there was no fire, but we weren't going any where that day.

They towed us back to the parking strip for repairs, but we soon found there were no spare wing tips other than back in Minneapolis and it would entaila 10 day layover.

This gave us many opportunities to tour Trinidad, (the land of the calypso.In fact one of our passengers, Lt."**Doc**" Ferrelle (from Savannah, Ga.) asked if I would like to fly around the area with him, in a Piper cub that he was able to borrow from an old acquaintance he ran into. Naturally I jumped at the chance and shortly we were flying low over a river in the jungle area.

We were about 500 feet above the river when he asked if I would like to take the controls for a while and he gave me a few quick instructions. He said "make a 90 degree turn and I immediately went into a 90 degree bank, which put the wings perpendicular to the river and is "not too smart" when only 500 Feet above a river any where, let alone in a jungle. He quickly righted the plane and let me continue to fly it and it was a really great experience.

We visited the small towns around the base to see what the native life was like and were literally amazed when we climbed into a native taxi. Though the driver was dressed in typical native clothing, he spoke impeccable english with an english accent you would find only in places like the universities. They put the London cabbies to shame, which I can verify as I later made many trips to London while flying the north Atlantic later on scheduled "Crescent Caravan" trips (that made 12 trips per day from the New Castle Air Base) via: Mitchell Field,(Long Island) Stephensville, (New Foundland) Reykjavik, (Iceland) or Lagens,.(Azores) into London or into Casablanca (Africa).

"Doc" and I were later to share a very memorable experience in India that I'll describe later. But during those ten days in Trinidad I started to grow a very scraggly goatee, which did little for my military appearance but, surprisingly enough, Captain Ackerman said not a word about either. We found a good deal on pith helmets in one of the towns and many of us bought them. still with no word from the left cockpit. After an

RON at Waller Field (Guyana) we landed in Belem, very picturesque, in the mouth of the Amazon River and surround on three sides by dense jungle. The river was loaded with pirhana, those little man eating fish that were only 5 inches long naturally none of us went swimming.

On our final stop in South America before the long haul over the ocean was at Natal, a little island about 100 miles off Recife, Brazil's shore. This would give us a little edge, fuel wise, on that long overwater flight into Accra.

We departed about 20:00 (8:00 local) as it would soon be dark and we wanted to use those southern hemisphere stars to guide us to the coast of Africa. As they "topped off" our fuel tanks to overflowing, I asked a captain in operations "what if get over halfway there and find we don't have sufficient fuel for the trip"? He said, "Just turn around and come on back". Ask a silly question and you get a silly answer.

But luck was running for this Irishman as it was a very clear night and all the stars I had selected were out in all their glory. This was my first chance to try out all of those skills that my instructors at Pan Am had so painstakingly pounded into my thick head.

Naturally I was quite nervous, but was doing my best to appear nonchalant in carrying out my assignment. The crew had no way of knowing that it was my first foreign trip, and I was not about to tell them how green I was. In fact I was quite concerned as to how they were accepting me as their "Magellan" who was to take them half way around the globe.

But this night everything fell into place as those myriads of instructions came to mind as needed. Even the sextant performed flawlessly and in my many years of flying I never had better shots or tighter triangles. Even my "cruise control" instructions worked well for me, in fact every thing went so I knew I had arrived as a celestial navigator.

Cruise control is quite important and it is (or was then) a navigators responsibility to keep track of the aircraft's weight and give the pilot throttle and prop pitch to match the weight drop for every 3,000 pounds of fuel used. As fuel weighed 7.5 pounds per gallon the plane became 3,000 pounds lighter for every 400 gallons we used. Cruise conrol also came into play if you lost an engine, or three as engines consume more fuel when they are under the strain of making up for a malfunctioning one and it we lose two the other two burn much more when trying to do the work of four engines.

We arrived in Accra early in the morning right on my eta, which resulted in a number of compliments from the crew. A strange thing about Accra is that due to the number of outdoor native markets that sold unrefrigerated meats was that the odor was so strong that we could actually smell them from the air as we made our approach.

After a short nap we made a quick tour of those markets and the odor was much stronger there. But that evening we attended an outdoor movie and another memorable incident occurred. I sat next to a young army corporal and asked him what his home town was? He replied, Pittsburgh, ˙Pa, Sir" and I said "so is mine".

So I asked him his name to which he replied "Dick Shoemaker, sir". Well it so happened that I was engaged to a Dorothy Shoemaker (my bride of 52 years). So I asked if he knew a Dorothy Shoemaker, to which he replied, "I have a sister named Dorothy". When I asked where in Pittsburgh he lived, "he said Shady Side and I knew he was my financee's brother.

On the surface this would sound great, but don't forget that I was dressed in "Bermuda shorts and shirt", wearing a pith helmet, natal boots and sporting (?) a very scraggly goatee. I never had a picture of that attire but years later my wife said that Dick had written her "that the war wouldn't last forever and don't be too hasty".

He never said a word but I did take him to the Officers club for a drink and that was the first and last time I would ever see him, as he died on Mindanao. The only time he was ever to see me was as a six foot one inch, very skinny idiot in that British shirt and short outfit, a pith helmet, natal boots and a very scraggly goatee.

Early the next morning as our crew was eating breakfast the base commander passed our table and asked who the aircraft commander was? When Captain Ackerman said "I am sir", the base commander said "Captain, before you leave this base that man will be clean shaven". So ended my short career as an Air Corps hippee, it's too bad that I didn't get to see Dick again while dressed as a normal crew member.

Our next stop was in Kano, Nigeria where there was a large "walled in" leper colony. We did see many lepers while there and it made you appreciate what you had as these people had large lesions on their faces, were missing toes and fingers. We all said many a silent prayer that night both for the lepers as well as in thanks for not being numbered among them.

In that area, around Lake Chad were large herds of elephants that were quite visible from the air as we passed over them and many other roving herds of animals native to that area.

We headed on to Khartoum, Egypt that was located on the Nile River, one of the few in the world that flows north. The Nile was quite beautiful with it's ancient buildings and it's scenic back ground, the native costumes, et al, in contrast to it's modern airbase. that we were using.

We still had 3 more stops before reaching our destination: Aden; in Arabia, Kurachi and Agra: in India, before the final long hop into Chabua. Each of those stops was unique in themselves, with it's own personality as Aden, in Arabia with it's arabic tongue, Kurachi and Agra, unlike the USA spoke several languages: many native dialects and english was well spoken in all the shops.

After leaving Kurachi we headed onto Agra, which was near New Delhi (the capital) and the home of the Taj Mahal, a most sacred edifice for the natives and most beautiful.

40

To tour the Taj Mahal cost us quite a few rupees, first you had to leave your shoes at the door and rent sandals, although a religious center. It was also a profit maker. It was divided into many sections and in each the visitors were required to leave donations. They also sold souvenirs and we were all loaded down upon exiting it.

All through Africa, Egypt, Arabia and India we were constantly amazed at the low prices of everything: food, clothing, jewelry, watches, ivory, copper plates, silver items, vases, scarves, etc., and we were exposed to a very different form of merchandising, vastly different from back home, especially the merchants in India.

The merchants would quote you a price on every item, that we later found to be three times the price they expected to sell it for. But even those prices were cheap to us and we would pay it, not realizing that we insulting him by not bartering with him. As we later found, they loved to haggle and lower their asking price, during which they would raise their voices when ever you quoted a lower price. When he looked like he was going to explode that was his final price and you had reached agreement with him.

As result of the crazy Americans buying everything at the initially quoted prices, though high to the natives, they were very reasonable to us and we would pay them. They had a price for the crazy Americans, a much lower one for the British colonials and a low,low price for the natives.

This made the British colonials very upset with us as the British military pay was much lower than the American military. Many of our enlisted were at the same level of many of the British officers, whose families were stationed there with them and quite dependent upon low prices. We were the cause of much inflation for those colonial families and they did not appreciate it..

After departing Agra we finally reached destination: Chabua, in the province of Assam, on the banks of the Brahmaputra river, which was infested with crocodiles.

Many natives had a custom of placing their dead on on rafts and floating them out into the river where eventually, the crocodiles would dispose of them or perhaps transport them to "Valhalla". But they had two forms of burial rites: Crocodiles and/or funeral pyres upon which the deceased were consumed by the flames.

Chabua had a single air strip built onto a tea plantation that was almost entirely surrounded by a jungle.In that jungle were orangutans, chimpanzees, monkeys, lions, tigers, cobras, russells vipers, coral snakes, and many other forms of animal life.

The airfield's landing strip had no lights, so there was no night flying, except in emergencies then trucks, jeeps, etc were lined on either side of the strip at angles facing away from the aircraft's flight path.

The buildings were all constructed of bamboo and had thatched rooves. The quarters, called bashas, officers and enlisted alike had exactly the same. Each had ten small rooms and in each room there were 3 cots under mosquito bars, that were hoisted to the ceiling during the day and dropped over the cots at night. Yes, the area was loaded with the anophele mosquito, a very prevalent source of malaria.

We had twice as many officers as enlisted due to the number of flight crews and administrative officers. This created problems as there were not sufficient enlisted to do all of the daily chores: K.P., guard duty, gassing & servicing the planes, truck driving, office work, cooking, etc.. etc..

It soon became apparent that the poor enlisted guys were being worked to death and had little time off. So a meeting was held, the situation explained and the officers were all "volunteered" by the base commandeer to walk sentry posts, do area policing (cleaning up the area) fueling the aircraft, office work and even K.P. on the days they were not flying.

We had only one officer, a 2nd. Lt. Silverman, refuse to "volunteer", so we held a kangaroo court and fined him $75 for every day he refused. At that time a second looey was only getting $125 a month and he couldn't afford to miss too many days and he eventually complied with the program.

The "Polo Grounds" was our living area and mess hall. It was about 1 1/4 miles from base ops and we either took the small jitney shuttle or walked back and forth. The largest building was the combination mess hall and "rec" center. It too, was constructed of bamboo and had a hatched roof. The kitchen was on one end, the dining area in the center and the recreation area was the far end plus the dining area.

The province of India in which we were located was Assam and though the enlisted men named the building as the "Assam Dragon" it was more a comment upon the amount of work they had to do daily, so the name of the "Assam Dragon Club" stuck.

Being at the far end of the military supply line that began in the states and wandered about 12,000 miles before reaching us, there wasn't much left in "the larder" by the time it reached us. We weren't exactly the best fed outfit in the military and much of the food had to be purchased locally from a nearby British Quartermaster. So we never had fresh meat of any kind, just canned corned beef and spam.

They were supplemented with powdered eggs, powdered potatos, powdered milk and a cheese you could not identify or eat, We had nothing that required refrigeration as we had little or no electricity (just a few small generators).

The flour for the bread was so loaded with insects, that for the first month or so, you wouldn't touch it, but soon you noticed everyone else simply help it up to the light and picked out the little critters and so did you shortly after.

Our cook had a one track mind, in that he would serve either spam, or corned beef, three times a day for a solid month and then switch to the other meat. He accompanied that meat with powdered scrambled eggs for breakfast, serve it as a sandwhich for lunch and hot for dinner with powdered mashed potatos.

We hadn't paid too much attention to food (as there was no other place to go) until it was reported that Gen. "Vinegar Joe" Stillwell (just out of a 3 month trek in the jungle) ate in in mess hall and got Ptomaine poisoning.

The "rec" hall was used by officers and enlisted for meetings, recreation, such a travelling troupe, or a rare movie, if you could locate a generator etc., as it was the only one space available. That included the nightly poker games but the really big ones were on payday. Those big games really proved to be a life saver for a fellow classmate..

"Kirk" Kirkpatrick, one of my classmates was on my plane on the way to India, as a passenger and the paymaster for both the passengers and the crew, which was the source of his woes. He was an inveterate, but lousy, gambler and every night enroute he would find a poker game and inevitably lose some of the governments money.

By the time he hit Chabua he was almost $3,000 in the hole and did not report into the finance office as he was supposed to up on arrival. He kept ignoring their messages and finally was given a deadline, which was the following Monday. Poor Kirk was going nuts as with him owing close to $3,000 with a monthly pay of about $125 he had problems.

But as luck would have it, he played one more time in the big Saturday night game, hit a lucky streak and won over $3,000. So early Monday morning he checked in with the finance officer and all was well. I wish I could say that he had learned his lesson but it wouldn't be true as he kept on looking for that silver lining and was always in debt.

As I said our airstrip was partly surrounded by a very densely populated jungle and many times we would see 14' cobras and pythons slithering along the runway, thusly creating a traffic hazard for landings and take offs. But we had a very dedicated medic who used them to our advantage. He was Corporal Dickinson who had been a curator of reptiles at the Long Beach Zoo in California. He captured many local varities of snakes and kept them in cages outside the entrance to the clinic. And as a dedicated scientist he would take their venom and devise a serum to counteract each one.

Then he would allow a certain snake to bite him, inject himself with his own serum to see how it worked. Eventually he perfected serums (sera?) to counteract each one of them and he reduced the hospital time for snake bite from two weeks to one day.

As you came to the clinic he would always hold out some variety of snake and say "hold it, it won't hurt you". He was right as I wouldn't get close enough for it to do so. I was and still am afraid of snakes. In fact one night as I was driving a jeep down that jungle road to "base ops" when I saw big Russell's viper on the road. I thought about running over it until I noticed how long it was and how close the jeep's floor board was to the ground, so I quickly swerved and went around it, not over it.

I was assigned the job of assistant group navigation officer, under group navigator Captain Daley. So I did the scheduling for all the navigators, including myself. Due to the number of days of bad flying weather in early April, all of the other navigators would watch the schedule very closely to see if I scheduled myself as often as they were. So I had to schedule myself more often than any one else.

You had to fly a mininum number of hours each month to collect flight pay and we had one officer who after flying the bare minimum would keep hitting "sick call" to get out of flying.

Guess who he was, yep he was the same one who refused to "volunteer" to help out the enlisted men. But I had a solution in that I knew Major Herring, the flight surgeon pretty well, so when I told him about Silverman's sick call routine he, Major Herring, said to me, "Lt. Kelly, He cain't get sick no more" in his Louisiana accent, and he didn't so I scheduled him in the worst weather I could find.

We weren't far from the western end of the Ledo Road (Burma Road) under construction and badly needed for the supplies for Chiang Kai Chek as we weren't able to fly all the needed supplies via planes.

The Ledo Road was part of the mountain range we flew over to Kunming and Chungking and the highest peak was Mt. Likiang that was listed on our charts at 17,000 ft. but I flew along side of it in the daylight at 23,000ft. It was nicknamed the "Aluminum plated mountain", due to the number of planes that hit it while flying on instruments, by pilots pilots who trusted the charts.

Although I was the assistant navigation officer I had not been alerted to the true altitude of it, but sure as heck I made sure every navigator knew it and they could alert the pilots to it.

Most of the time we were on instruments but on a clear day the view was breathtaking. High mountains with snow on them, deep valleys of green jungle and it was like reading a road map. There was the West Irrawaddy, the East Irrawaddy, the Salween and the Mekong rivers and of course Mt. Likiang.

Kunming was about 6,000 feet high and it made for hot landings at that thin air and the runways were of crushed crushed rock. This made for several problems, hot landings, fast take offs and flying bits of crushed rock that penetrated the fuselage and tail surfaces flying up from the wheels.

Kunming was the headquarters of the most famous flier in the world Gen. Claire Chennault of Flying Tiger fame. He was however, not in the good graces of the other general officers, both of whom outranked him: Gen. Clayton Bissell, the Theatre commander and Gen "Vinegar Joe" Stillwell ground forces commander.

Stillwell and Bissell both hated Chennault as well as Chiang Kai Chek as, Chennault, and the Generalissimo were in the good graces of President Roosevelt. In fact in one meeting in Washington, D.C. with Chennault, himself and the President he, Stillwell, lost his temper and insulted Chiang Kai Chek and never recovered from that embarrassment.

Bissell, though the theatre commander, had his headquarters in New Delhi, many thousand miles to the west and no where near the war zone. He did his best to work in conjunction with Stillwell and against Chennault by delaying needed materials, etc.. The tension got so bad that Chennault's outfit (14th. A.F.) took such a dislike for Bissell that they arranged a special greeting for him.

So, on his next visit to Kunming, a large group of Chinese natives and troops filled the area around base-ops and when Bissell debarked from his plane the Chinese, in loud, clear voices, greeted him with "Piss on Bissell Piss on Bissell". They kept bowing and chanting what they thought was a proper greeting not realizing they had been coached phonetically as they knew no english.

Bissell was outraged, but of course no one knew who was responsible and naturally Chennault was **quite horrified** that anyone would do such a thing.

One quirk of nature was discovered while flying the hump, the "jet stream". One of the first instances involved a friend of mine, Captain Spurlock, while piloting a C-46 that was fully loaded with cargo.

The weather wasn't very co-operative that day and he was in and out of clouds constantly. Being the cautious pilot that he was, he decided to give himself as much leeway with the ridges as possible and climbed a little higher. Very shortly into that climb his plane suddenly flipped upside down.

Can you imagine your anything more frightening than to find yourself upside down in a fully loaded C-46, on instruments, and trying to figure out what had happened? It took him some time to acclimate himself while hanging from his seat belt, indicating 170 mph, at 20,000 feet.

He later said it was almost terrifying as his controls were now working in reverse. To climb he would have to push the stick forward, to descend he would have to pull back and to bank left he would have to move the controls right. In desperation he tried a reverse chandelle and it righted the aircraft so he did a 180 and headed back for the Chabua.

Immediately, upon landing he said, "I've had it, no more flying for me". The operations officer, Captain Hugh Wild, went along with him, gave him ground assignments like driving the fuel trucks to fuel the planes, but in about a month he was back flying again.

While others had discovered some peculiarities at upper levels they eventually discovered those strong air currents but how they determined what it was I never knew.

Speaking of the C-46's they had just switched from electric props to the conventional and were having problems with them in addition to the firewall problem. There was no firewall and any leaking fuel that came in contact with a hot engine would ignite.

The CAA had recommended 622 modifications as necessary before they could be used by the general public, but we were given them to fly on the hump. The prop problem was a serious as when it "ran away" it had to be feathered and at 18 to 20,000 feet the C-46 could not maintain altitude on one engine.

This resulted in one of the largest airsearches we ever had in the CBI when Eric Sevareid (noted correspondent) was aboard the C-46 piloted by two young lieutenants: Lts.Felix and Spain, a radio operator, flight engineer and 19 passengers enroute to Kunming. Not too long after take-off, while over the hills of Burma, a prop failed and they all had to bail out.

They all managed to leave the plane, but the co-pilot had stayed at the controls til everyone else exited but the plane was so close to the ground when he left and his chute failed to open. He did manage to radio a "mayday" before doing so and the base was alerted. Base ops immediately sent up four C-47's, each assigned a different sector to search.

Fortunately for me, the pilot I was assigned to, was the one who had let me fly that Piper Cub around the jungles of Trinidad "Doc" Ferrelle. It was early in the afternoon before we were airborne and each plane had a few emergency kits and rations put onboard to drop to them if we sighted them as they had no food, warm clothing, rain gear or portable radios.

We had kits to drop that contained material to be laid out on the ground to identify the condition of each passenger or crew member. It contained written instructions of how to place markers on the ground that listed them as to the number assigned on the manifest that was in the kit. For example after the numeral one (first passenger listed) they would place a large check mark if he was ok, a large "x" if he were deceased and a "?" if injured.

After searching our area for several hours we came over a high ridge and there was a large valley, almost in was no was no room for a plane to land and helicopters were a thing of the future.

To drop into that valley close enough to drop materials and to the shape of a bowl with sides up around 9,000 feet and the ends up around 8,000. We immediately spotted a number of parachutes spread out in the bottom of the bowl but couldn't see any signs of movement. There read those markers "Doc" had to use half flaps, reduce power then full power and full flaps and chug back up out of there. Then he had to repeat that procedure to read each marker after dropping them the supplies and instructions, he made at least 30 drops down into that valley.

After making a head count we found that only one had not made it, Lt. Felix, as we were later to learn his chute did not open. Most were ok but there were a few injuries but it was getting late and, as we had no night landing facilities, we headed on back before it got dark. First we dropped them a note that we would return in the morning with medics and more supplies.

Since we were the plane that found them we were the crew that would monitor the rest of their stay until they were picked up via ground vehicles.

So early next morning we loaded those supplies, the flight surgeon (Maj. Herring), three medics who would jump into the valley with him and a two way portable radio to make verbal contact with them to find their needs.

Also on board was a new co-pilot, a Captain M.M. Jones, from Group H.Q. as they were very interested in Mr. Sevareid's welfare. Major Herring would carry the portable radio with him and Captain Jones would monitor it from the plane. And when it was tuned in, after Major Herring and the medics had landed ok, Captain Jones asked if there was any thing in particular they wanted. The answer was "Fried chicken and ice cream".

As I had previously mentioned that our mess hall had only canned or dehydrated foods I though these guys were hallucinating. But Captain Jones said he would give it a try. Early the next morning a Major Katz, also from Group H.Q., replaced Jones as the co-pilot, and he had several ice chests with him, tied to their own little parachute and they were loaded "believe it or not" with "fried chicken and ice cream" from General Alexander's residence. It was immediately apparent they ate better than we did.

With helicopters unheard of, no landing strips or roads nearby that party, they would have to walk out to where ever ground transportation could get close enough to pick them up. They had to trek almost 50 mile to a spot where several trucks picked them up, it took about a week.

They were monitored along the way but that was the last time "Doc" Ferrelle or I would be involved with them and it was over two years later that the Readers Digest gave Sevareid's version of that incident. Neither "Doc" nor I were ever mentioned. But after "Doc" doing all of that skillful flying I was hoping he would get some credit.

That wasn't the only adventure incorrectly reported as we had a pilot named Captain Bill Cherry who has been on that famous flight of Captain Eddie Rickenbacker's in which their B-17 ditched in the ocean and they survived for several days in life rafts before being rescued.

Rickenbacker had been credited for saving them via taking care of the food to see it lasted. He was also credited with having a seagull land on his shoulder whether they ate it or not I don't recall.

But Bill Cherry said Rickenbacker was a big phoney and they had to keep the food away from him. While he and Rickenbacker were making war bond tours, Cherry kept complaining about Rickenbacker being a phoney and it was starting to hinder the war bond tour. So the Pentagon decided to keep Cherry quiet by shipping him to the far off CBI theatre where I met him.

The reason Cherry disliked Rickenbacker was that prior to the takeoff the navigator had dropped his sextant on the tarmac. When he wanted to take it back to the operations office to replace it, Rickenbacher said "no". And the theory is that is why they got lost because of a broken sextant that Rickenbacker wouldn't waste time to get a replacement for it.

We had another pilot also "shanghaied" to our theatre to get him out of the public eye. He was Tommy Harmon the famous football player who crashed landed a B-25 in the

Jungles of Brazil and he was the only survivor. A rumor stared that he had bailed out and left the rest of the crew to crash.

Now anyone who has ever flown in a B-25 knows it's an impossibility to exit without the knowledge and help of he other crew members. To get out the top you had to stand on the navigator's table and go out the top hatch right in beween two twirling props which, if you were fortunate to pass, then there was that razor sharp antenna stretched between the two vertical stabilizors that cut cut you in half. Or you could ask the bombardier to get up and let you out his escape hatch, but I doubt it if he would let the pilot out while he remained on board. But the damage was done and Harmon had a bad press, so he was hurriedly checked out on P-38's and shipped to China. I got to meet him during his layover in Chabua when he went to see our chaplain, Father King.

Tommy was seeking advice about his upcoming marriage to an actress named Elyse Knox who was a divorcee, but as a non-catholic, not married by a priest, her marriage was not recognized by the Church and he was free to wed her, which he did upon his return to the states.

Tommy was no slouch in that P-38 as I had told him that when transient crews left our base they would make a low pass over our barracks area at the Polo grounds. Well, when Tommy left he put all of those other pilots to shame as he flew so low between our bashas he could have literally picked up a hankerchief off the ground with his wing tip.

He was still at our base when one of the enlisted tower operators committed suicide by putting a gun in his mouth and pulling the trigger. I remember seeing Tommy open the back door of the ambulance and pulling the sheet off of the young man to see what he looked like.

I wasn't the least bit interested. I had seen all of the dead crew members I cared to see on Good Friday shortly before when a series of incidents occurred on our air strip.

The first of which was a C-87 that on take offf had veered off the runway and cut right through a C-47 on a taxi strip and killed the pilot and co-pilot of the C-47. A crewman asleep in it's tail section received a nasty shock when he woke up unharmed.

It seemed the crew chief on the C-87 had forgotten to pull the rudder and elevator locks leaving the pilot with no lateral control of the plane on the runway.

I was the A.O. (aerdrome officer) and one of the first on the scene. When we extinguished the flames we found both the pilot and co-pilot strapped in their harness but, the arms and legs were burned off of each of them.

While that was happening a B-24 called in that he was on final approach, but he crashed a mile short of the runway, with no survivors. It was really a very somber Good Friday.

There's an old superstition that these thing happen in threes and shortly after Denny Beasely, who was one of our nicest pilots got his orders to go home. The plane he left for home own crashed on the way to Bombay and poor Denny did not survive.

Tony Donabedian, whom I had flown the hump with many times, told me that he had a premonition that he would never leave the hump alive. Sad to say he was correct as on a subsequent trip to Kunming he never returned nor was his plane ever found.

We had a higher attrition rate on the hump than the 10th and 14th A.F.'s had in combat but we did have our own bombardier, Clyde Sarver a transport pilot who scrounged bombs from friends in the 14th. A.F. Then he would fly over a Japanese airstrip in Burma (called Sumpra Bum) and kick his bombs out of his cargo door, hoping to hit some thing.

He wasn't in any danger as the Japs only used that that base occasionally. They would fly some bombers in just before dark, then in the early morn they would take off, head for our area and then return to their base somewhere in Burma or Japan. We were not equipt for nite flying, nor was their base in Sumpra Bum. It was just a harassing tactic and never of any major proportion, just to keep us alert as Sarver did to them.

They had another way of keeping us on edge as they were great on infiltrating our area and they would sneak into our basha at night and slash the throat of just one occupant of a room of three. When the other two awoke and found that one of them was dead and it could have been them, it really had an impact and kept, not only those two, but every one in the basha (and nearby bashas) felt quite unsafe for days on end knowing it could happen again quite easily.

We had the pleasure of meeting several of Doolittle's Tokyo Raiders on their return to states via our area.. The two I remember were Major "Butch" Halstrom and Lt. Young blood, both of whom I was later to meet at a Doolittle convention. There was as Brig. Gen. Casey Vincent, known as the boy general as he was only 29 the youngest in the Air Corps, an excellent pilot, a respected commander, a survivor of the 14th. A.F.'s high attrition rate they had earlier in the war. I was later to meet him again when I was flying the north Atlantic route and when in Reykjavik, Iceland I accidently walked into his quarters at the BOQ.

There was another gentleman who was also a victim, or should I say beneficiary, of that attrition rate. I had met a second lieutenant from my home town of Pittsburgh, Pa.

He was Butch Morgan who had graduated from Carnegie-Tech, (same school my fiancee attended). He passed through Chabua in April and the next time I saw him was in September and he was a Major on his way home.

There were many facets about flying the hump, it wasn't just that you had to fly over a large mountain range taking needed materials to aid somewhat in the conflict with Japan. It was the manner in which you lived when you were not flying: the ever present possibility of contracting malaria, be bitten by a poisonous snake, attacked by a wild animal, have your throat slit while in bed, encountering bad weather in the air, or an enemy plane, but there was another one that could possibly prey on your mind.

Due to the number of headhunters who lived in the jungles we wore both a Chinese flag on the back of our A-2 flying jackets, as well as a message that we carried a money money belt with rupees in it and it was theirs (the head hunters) if they left our heads intact or didn't turn us over to a roving Japaneze patrol.

Another hazard that faced any crew member that had the misfortune to bail out was the combination of wild animals and the snakes were those leeches that were quite large and even more terrifying than the animals and snakes.

The only way to remove them was by applying a lit cigarette butt to them causing them to back out of the skin. As they would literally cover all exposed areas of the body they almost impossible for one person to remove them. Anyone who had to spend any time in those wet jungles it was indeed a nightmare and not too many managed to walk out.

The terrain was also against anyone traveling on the ground as it consisted of many hills and valleys. To walk a mile horizontally it meant almost 3 to 4 miles vertically.

I recall one survivor who had spent many long nights in our infirmary after several weeks in the jungle. He was almost completely out of his head. He'd wake up screaming "Get them off of me get them off of me". He was almost a "psycho case", mostly due to the leeches.

As we had no laundry facilities we had to depend upon he wives of the native workers to do our washing. This was done by washing them in the river and beating them on the rocks. In order to identify whose clothes they were washing they would mark them with betel nut juice inside the collar of the shirts or the in seam of the trouser, underwear, etc. usually an area that touch the skin when wearing them, much to our regret.

The native women liked to chew betel nuts whose juice was a deep purple color that stained the areas around their mouths giving them all a most peculiar appearance. While it didn't appear to affect them otherwise, it sure did affect all of us in that it created rashes where it came in contact with the skin and it caused large blisters that would spread across wide areas of the body.

The only thing the dispensary had to counteract those large blisters was jensens violet that also was deep purple in color. As those blisters would cover large areas of our arms, legs, backs, necks, stomaches, etc., and we had to literally cover them with jensens violet we soon looked like a lot of circus clowns. As I said malaria was quite rampant there due to the large numbers of the anopheles mosquitos in the area, so we were always being fed both atrabine and salt tablets.

The main part of our day seemed to be spent in our mess hall as we had to visit it at least 3 times a day to eat or to pass the time away in the evenings. I keep harping on the quality of the food (or the lack of it's quality) due to it's dependence on dehydrated or powdered foods.

Though there were vegetables available in the nearby village of Chabua, the flight surgeon would not allow the cook to use them due to the number of local diseases combined with the fact the local farmers used human excrement for their fertilizers which made those vegetable literally dynamite for us to eat. While the natives had built in immunity to those diseases, we didn't and the flight surgeon knew it..

We weren't far from the Ledo Road and there were a number of British families living there: tea plantation owners, military families, etc. In fact both Gen. Chennault and the Generalissimo had friends there and would occasionally fly in to visit with them. Despite they many rumors that each had lady friends there, we had no way of proving it or even caring whether they did or not. But if you were on duty as the A.O. or working with transient crews you invariably met them.

As I had been a classmate of Peter Chu, who was the Generalissimo's nephew I was looking forward to meeting him. I did get the opportunity to tell him that I was acquainted with his nephew who was now a Colonel in the Chinese Air Force.

Due to the nearness of the Jap base at Sumpra Bum we had an alarm system set up to warn us of their approach.

How ever with no electicity to sound an alarm there was what was known as the "red ball Alert" system. There were high polls around the area, each with three small arms on them to which would be large red balls attached in case of an alarm: If only one ball it meant Jap aircraft were in the over all area, but not us. If two balls it meant nearby bases but if it were three balls it was for us.

But we never had to wait for a three ball alert as the natives had a better "grape vine" than we did and, before any three ball red alert were raised, they would be long gone. So as soon as there was a sudden shortage of natives you knew something was up.

Speaking of Jap attacks, we had a number of slit trenches dug out in a field not too far from the mess hall that we were to dive into, after you looked for snakes. Now no one in their right mind wants to bring the enemy attention to you area, but we had a really bright Major who supervised our compound. He had those slit trenches dug out in the shape of his initials, one was a huge "H", one a large "L" and the other a big "T". Combined it was a great big "H-L-T" that could be seen from miles away in the air. It stood for Harold L. Townsend who was "really looking out for us".

We lived in bashas and each of us had a houseboy or "Bapu" who took care of our rooms, clothes, beds, mosquito bars, etc., We tipped them every week with a rupee or a few annas which wasn't much to us, but though a rupee was only around 75 cents at the time, my bapu told me his father made only 75 rupees per year at his job.

But back to the bapu to whom I was speaking to or perhaps yelling at, when a

British major walked by who I had met before. He heard my "discussion" and said to me "Lt. Kelly, you are evidently confident in your military capabilities", to which I agreed.

He then said, "you obviously feel you are more intelligent than that native boy who works for you"? Again I answered in the affirmative, to which he replied "then why don't you speak to him in his language"? He said my class_on Urdu commences at 7:00 P.M. tonite. Needless to say I_was there, and while I managed to learn a little Urdu like "garum pani" and "tanda pani" to order hot or cold tea, I never became the linquist Major Haas was.

You often hear of thievery by the natives in foreign lands but not in our area of India, we had little, if any, of it as you could leave anything you had lying out in the open in your room and it would be there when you return. I hate to say it but those natives were more to be trusted than our own people were.

There was alway some kind of a ball game going on during the day light hours, even during the monsoon season when it really poured down 2 or 3 times a day. But the sun was so hot that it took only minutes to dry up the playing field. In fact some of the games were scheduled for after the first or second rains.

I particularly remember one baseball game where the officers were playing against the enlisted and, as usual, there were no holds barred, we played for blood. I was catching for the officers' team when a man on first broke for second as the batter swung at a pitch and he missed. I had gotten my middle finger in the catchers mitt before the ball got there and broke it. I made the throw to second in time to throw him out before I noticed the bone sticking out of my finger. I hadn't felt any pain but needless to say I didn't finish the game.

That wasn't my first trip to the dispensary as several months prior I had a pilonidal sinus, or a cyst on the base of the spine. Major Herring, flight surgeon, removed it and secured a rest leave for me after the operation. He recommended that I spend it in Darjeeling, high in the Himalaya's and across a ravine from Mt. Everest.

To get there you had to fly to Calcutta, take a train from there to the little village of Siliguri at the base of the Himalayas. Then via, a very tiny guage railway climb 7,000 feet up the mountains to Darjeeling.

That little railway was, at the time, listed as one of the seven wonders of the world for the unique manner in which it climbed up that mountain. It utilized a system known as "switch backs" in which the train would get up a full head of steam and climb a fairly long steepgrade until it couldn't make any more headway and then back the train into a siding.

These had been pre-calculated so there would be a switch at which the train could back into a fairly long siding. Once back into the end of that siding the engineer would get up another full head of steam and take off again up another fairly long slope until he reached the next switchback and so on until they reached Darjeeling 7,000 feet up the mountain.

Sometimes, when there were too many passengers the train couldn't quite make it to the next switch. When that occurred many of the passengers would get off and walk to the next switch back to make it easier for the engineer.

Darjeeling was a beautiful city, high on top of the Himalayas directly across the ravine from Mt. Everest, with a very spectacular view. It was listed as "the home of the world's finest tea", there were several beautiful hotels and the food was wonderful. It was patterned after London as so many British either live or frequently visited there.Many were families of high ranking military who could afford it, but There weren't many tourists as it was too remote.

We did get to Calcutta occasionally and they way we did it was via the "basket leave" program. If you could wangle some time off and wanted to go to Calcutta, or other nearby areas that we flew to, you made out a leave request, put it in the basket at base ops and when a plane was heading the direction you wanted you simply hopped on board. If during the time you were gone no one was looking for you to pull duty, then you simply removed your leave request and it did not count against your official leave time.

At that time there was a huge famine in Calcutta, too many for the local authorities to handle. So every morning you would see many dead bodies lying in the streets awaiting to be picked up by British lorries and hauled off to a funeral pyre for disposal. It was not uncommon to see huge rats scurrying about the streets, as well as large boa constrictors slithering around the streets looking for those rats, as a form of rat control.

There were many beggars roaming the streets, many of them women, who would rub their stomaches while crying out "Sahib, no papa, no mama, little one inside, baksheesh" which meant gift please.

Many natives carried burlap sacks, one of which would carry a mongoose and the other a cobra and for a few annas they would put them on the street were they would let the mongoose fight the cobra, not to death as that was the way they made a living. An anna was half a rupee, or about 37 cents, then they had pice and pi which where like our nickels and dimes but as forementioned 75 rupees were almost annual wages for the natives.

The British have been accused of exploiting India, but I think they did much for the country and the natives as a whole, in that they helped industrialize them in addition to protecting them, military wise, from surrounding nations with views of expansion. They helped them set up their railway system, showed them how to develope tea plantations, use looms to weave cloth and pursue many arts that enabled them to establish their own shops.

Back to the hump where I had hired out my sextant, we were near the Burma border and in the distance we saw see the beautiful hills of the Himalayas, even while not flying over them. They were a constant reminder that, as beautiful as they were, you could not relax while flying that approximately 3 hour 500 mile hop into Kunming as Mother Nature could be awful deceitful at times and the clear weather could change almost instantly to deep soup.

That was one of the reasons Mt. Likiang was called the "Aluminum Plated" mounted as with no visibility and the maps listing it at 17,000 feet though actually it's peak was 23,000 feet that I verified on a clear day.

If flying a C-87 or a C-46 you could reach 23,000 if you weren't too heavily loaded, but not so with a C-47, so if on a C- 47 you steered well south of Likiang in bad weather, where there was alway a greater chance of encountering enemy planes, but you would not add any aluminum to the hillside.

In the last 6 months of 1943 we were operating out of 4 bases in upper Assam: Chabua, Dinjan, Jorhat and Sookerating and we lost only 6 transports to enemy action, not anywhere in comparison to the 135 aircraft and over 179 crew men lost due to weather, mechanical difficulties, or accidents, which were the combined totals listed for those 4 bases.

I almost forgot about a not too well known rank for flying personnel, that of flying sergeants, of which we had two at Chabua, one of which Staff Sgt. Plummer. The program had begun in 1941 when I was on manuevers with the 176th Field Artillery in the Carolina, coincidentally as a Staff (platoon) sergeant.

When we returned to Fort Meade from those maneuvers I immediately went to the main post to apply for the flying sergeant program, only to find I was several months too old. But the sergeant at the main post said, "hold on to your papers and take them to "Division Hill" where they had announced the "aviation cadet" program. I took his advice that eventually led to"hiring out my sextant" via that program.

We had several flying sergeants and the Air Corps wanted to upgrade them and decided on the "warrant officer" rank making them neither officer nor enlisted, they were in between which created more problems: would they be billeted and/or fed as officers or enlisted?

But back to staff sergeant Plummer he was already getting mixed up. When not flying he was enlisted, lived in their barracks and ate in their mess, but when flying he was treated like an officer as he was an aircraft commander. As the aircraft commander he loved to order Captains and Lieutenants to remain on board the plane while he (Plummer) went into the operations office where it was slightly cooler. But his co-pilot, no matter his rank, had to take "Sergeant" Plummers orders and stay on board that sweltering aircraft in the 100 degree weather.

To overcome those problems an order came that permitted those flying sergeants to apply for warrant officer or second lieutenant. Plummer had a lot more flight time than some of our captains so he refused the warrant officer and second lieutenant ranks, holding out for captain or nothing. When I left there in

December of '43 I heard he was still a staff sergeant, but making it very miserable on his commissioned co-pilots.

The Air Transport Commander was B. Gen. Edward Alexander who, as a colonel established the hump operation in the summer of 1942 with just a few C-47's and C-87's (that B-24 cargo version) and at best, were hauling about 4,000 tons a month but they soon received the C-46 Curtiss Commando twin engine planes that could carry a 5,000 pound payload as against the C-47's 4,000 pounds, was faster and capable of higher altitudes.

Although they were only managing 4,000 tons in late '42 the arrival of the C-46's soon boosted that and by the end of '43, as I was heading home, it was up over 12,000 tons per month. A good showing but still not enough to keep Chiang Kai Chek and Chennault in business, which is why so much emphacise was being placed on finishing the Ledo Road.

To fly the hump they recommended using oxygen above 10,000 feet. We found it possible, with no bad affects, that we didn't have to use it until 18,000 feet. However one of us always wore a mask, just in case. Many times the pilots left their windows open to feel the cool air, but above 18,000 feet that was just a little too cold.

As there wasn't too much for a navigator to do in clear weather as you were merely map reading and on instruments it was mainly dead reckoning and/or the radio. So the pilots would let you pick up some stick time in the co-pilot's seat. In fact we had several navigators become so proficient that they checked them out as pilots and eventually received a pilots rating.

As mentioned those four rivers: west Irrawaddy, east Irrawaddy, the Salween and the Mekong, along with Mt. Likiang made for excellent map reading. Likiang wasn't as high as Mt. Everest, but Everest was so far north we seldom saw it.

In north central Burma was a settlement named Myetkina but pronounced "Mish-a-na" and the Army had a ground post there and were constantly patrolling that country for Japs as well as keeping an eye out for any crews that had bailed out or were missing. I had a brother-in-law (an army engineer) stationed there the year after I left as his out fit was sent to speed up completion of the Ledo Road. A funny thing happened about 15 years later at a family function back in Pittsburgh, Pa..

We were telling war stories and he was describing some of India's and Burma's native's customs. He told us of a great feast the native women had prepared for their outfit, with many delicacies, especially a soft food that was served to them.

He did not know how those meat dishes were prepared until I informed him that with no electricity, or mixing machines, that all of those food were "pre-chewed" by the native women. Although it was 15 years since he had eaten that food, immediately burst for the bathroom and threw up talk about a delayed reaction.

The reason I knew how the were prepared was that a British captain, who I met on my trip to Darjeeling, warned me not to eat any of those foods (when the train stopped) at all those of those towns along the tracks where you could get off to get a bite to eat. That was why, when the British and/or the wealthier Indians families travelled they carried their own foods with them.

Lord Louis Montbatten was the top British Commander in the area and he had a room set aside for him in one of our bashas. As he seldom came without advanced notice we used his room to hold parties. I recall one time when one of our pilots brought his pet tiger cub while others even had pet monkeys (that they even took with them on their flights).

At the party some one put saucers on the floor with lot of beer and alcohol in them and it wasn't long til we had a drunken tiger cub and and a few tipsy monkeys running around. Some of Lord Louie's glasses were being tossed around by inebriated crewmen who were also reciting poetry while throwing glasses against the walls which were of bamboo and the ceilings were thatched. Some of the basha had cement floor to keep out burrowing animals and Lord Louie had one of them, which is why the glasses were breaking.

Being at the far end of the supply line we had very few toilet articles, beer, wine or liquor, but occasionally some kind hearted crew members knew that and would bring some into us. Eventually some of those items began to trickle in as the enlisted didn't have the opportunities to pick them up in one of the bigger cities.

So we eventually began to receive regular monthly rations of beer and liquor. As yet I didn't drink, so I was quite popular at the ration times as I would give mine to my friends, of whom I had quiet a few over there, including 10 classmates from navigation school, plus a lot of pilots and other crew members you flew with. The liquor we received was usually Canadian club and that the first brand I ever drank. Having no electricity, no refrigereration or ice cubes the only mix available was canned grapefruit juice. So you either drank warm beer or a warm glass of Canadian Club and grape fruit juice.

But we had some real dedicated drinkers who wouldn't let a little thing like that deter them. Speaking of characters, we had our share of them and being far from Calcutta and other large towns there was little female company around. So many of them became color blind and made friends with some of the local native girls who, to them, got whiter by the day.

Naturally some of them picked up venereal diseases and this resulted in some unfair practices at the clinic as the officers went into the records as "colds" while the poor enlisted guys went into the official records as "venereal diseases". R.H.I.P once again had reared it's ugly head.

Our operations officer was a top flight officer, pilot and gentleman, just a heckuva nice guy to be around and to work with. We all took turns as the Aerdrome Officer or

'A.O.' who handled all the transient complaints, oversaw the work in base ops, patrolled the flight line, the refueling area, etc.

Though he didn't have to, he also took a regular turn as the 'A.O.', took regular trips over the hump, on searches, etc. I was reading a book about the hump about ten years ago and in it the author very sadly wrote that "Captain HughWild" got caught in a down draft and was killed.

Shortly after reading that I went to an A.F.A. State Convention and I ran into him. I said "Hugh, don't you know you're not supposed to be here as I just read that you were dead".

He said it was news to him and as Mark Twain had said about his own death report "That it was greatly exaggerated". In actuality Hugh had retired as a Brig. Gen. and was now the head of the water department in Tacoma, Wa. I later sent him the copy of that book.

Speaking of the duties of the 'A.O.', I was out patrolling the runway when I notice a B-24 approaching the run way flying low and fast with a lot of articles falling out of it's bomb bay area and I could actually see into the bomb bay whose doors were missing.

It was going much too fast for a normal landing and had no flaps down. At the far end of the runway was a large rainage ditch, about fifteen feet long, four feet wide and about several feet deep. The plane didnt slow or stop until it went into the ditch and the fuselage buckled with it's nose and tail on the ground and the center of the fuselage up in the air.

The pilot hopped out and ran for the trees, but fortunately a Captain came rushing up in a jeep with several fire extinguishers and we began spraying the nose section as there was some one in it. The bombardier as we later found, he was under a load of baggage and odds and ends, but luckily he was ok as were the rest of the crew, who we helped out.

Fortunately there were only minor injuries but we soon heard a strange, but sad tale, from the survivors who were looking for five other men. It seems that the plane had only landed a few hours ago after about a 10 day trip from the states, piloted by a Lieutenant Horne, who wanted to take an orientation flight around the area. He asked the ground crew if they would like to take a hop around the area. Now ground crews get very few opportunities to fly, so five of them said "yes" and hopped aboard.

He put them in the fuselage area and took off to see the area. He was flying very low and decided to give them all a thrill by buzzing the Bramaputra River. He had not yet learned that the B-24 doesn't react like a fighter plane that responds instantly to the controls.

The B-24 tends to mush (or sink) before responding to the signal to climb so when he got close to the river surface and pulled back on the stick, the plane dropped a little prior to responding, but he was a little too close to the water and the plane hit it. Hitting water at that speed is like hitting concrete and it tore the entire bottom out of the fuselage, the entire bombay was torn out with those 5 ground crew members who were ground to bits.

Even if they hadn't been they still wouldn't have survived as the river was loaded with crocodiles. In fact the local natives used to place their deceased upon rafts and floated them out on to the river where the crocodiles finished the funeral ceremony.

Yes, Lieutenant Horne had spent almost two weeks enroute, via the same route we had taken, to bring a badly needed aircraft to the 14th.A.F. and in just a few hours he did more damage to our group than the enemy had done in months. He cost the war effort the use of an expensive, badly needed air plane. He cost his squadron the use of his skills but even worse he cost us, and five families the loss of five skilled men who were dearly missed by their families, all needlessly.

Everything on the flight lines weren't always that serious, a p-40 pilot of the 14th A.F., (who I had met in the hospital) called in to the tower in Kunming requesting a "single engine landing ".

Naturally the tower assumed it was a two engine plane that had lost an engine and immediately called out the fire truck and emergency equipment only to have a single engined fighter plane land.

My friend, Lt. George Colarich really got chewed out by the operations office and the base commander, but he did break up the monotony that day. I met him in the hospital after he had walked out of the jungle where he had spent about a week to ten days following a bail out.

Another day, while serving as the 'A.O.' I was in a hurry to get a ride to the Polo grounds for a quick lunch after a very busy morning. As I came off the runway into base-ops I saw the jitney bus getting ready to take off. I called out to the driver to hold it up a minute as I had to run into base ops to dropoff some paperwork.

The driver replied, "I can't,sir" to which I, as a big second lieutenant, said, "you will wait and that's an order". About two minutes later I came out and climbed aboard only to notice in a rear seat was our commanding officer B.-Gen. Alexander sitting there. Neither he, nor any one else, said a word in the longest five minute ride in my life.

The months began to roll by and it was late in November when we received word that that a number of us, including many of my classmates, had garnered sufficient points to earn a return to the states as soon as replacements arrived. Finally in mid December we were given orders to fly to Kurachi, about 1,500 miles to the west, to fine transportation home. There weren't many flights available but we did hear that a passenger ship, the S.S. Lurline, would be pulling out of Bombay in in few days and we could book passage on it if we took that narrow guage train from Kurachi to Bombay.

We found it would take 3 days, so we called the office in Bombay see if we could book passage as it would take us three days to get there. They were most co-operative and assured us the ship would still be there when we arrived. That sounded like a good deal to us and we bought tickets for that train trip.

The rail cars, like the one I took to Darjeeling, were the small four man cars with two long bunks on either side, two hanging from the ceiling and two several feet above floor level During the day we sat, two on each side facing the center of the car, but at night each one had his own bunk.

The cars had a little platform at one end of each, they were about 4 feet long and ran the width of the car. That is where the native servants of the wealthy Indians who traveled on the train. The kept large containers of food to be served to their employers along the way.

Three of us: Lt. Marty Scheinkman. of New York City, Lt. George Kirkpatrick, of Pittsburgh, Pa., and I (all classmates from the Pan Am school) were assigned to a car that already had one passenger, a very distinguished one. He was the Maharajah of the province of Cooch Behar, a large area near Assam. He was enroute to some big event in Bombay and had several servants on the little covered porch with his food for the trip.

He and I sat on one side facing Scheinkman and Kirk Patrick. This would prove quite beneficial to me during the three day trip. Yes, it was only around 500 miles, but it did take three days travel time. As it was very hot we kept the windows open all the time, which also was to help me.

The Maharajah did his best to be a perfect host to those American Officers who were helping keep the Japanese out of his country. At each stop his servants brought those casks of food and beverages to him. some of them looked very exotic, including those soft meats I previously referred to.

With my two companions sitting opposite of us they could not refuse his hospitality and had to eat everything his servants placed before them. But they hadn't heard how the food was prepared anyhow.

Fortunately by sitting along side of the Maharajah with my back to an open window I could secretly discard anything I didn't care to eat. It was a most enjoyable three days and we all exchanged addresses with the Maharajah who invited us to come to his home anytime we were in his area.

We reached Bombay right on schedule and caught a taxi immediately to the dock where the S.S. Lurline was berthed. It was a luxury cruise ship that the Navy had taken over and kept the civilian crew to operate it but with a navy complement to over see it.

We were assigned cabins on the top deck that opened up to little patios for each cabin and there were four passengers to each cabin. In addition to the ten of us from the hump there were a number of Navy enlisted who had been in the Phillipines when the Japs over ran it. They had been based but not on sea going assignments but did manage to find a way to India and hopefully the states.

There were also 1,500 Italian prisoners of war on board heading to Australia to work in the fields on the prison farms. There were a number of British Army enlisted under one officer, and Irish Major who was tough as nails.

The prisoners were quartered in the hold, decks below where it was as hot as Hades. They were allowed to come up to the top decks occasionally, if properly supervised.

If they became unruly the Major and his men treated them very roughly. In fact the Major had asked the ship's commander for permission to "spread eagle" and flog them if they got out of hand. The Navy Captain refused, telling him that flogging went out of the U.S. Navy in 1889.

Now the rest part of the trip for us was that the ship had fresh vegetables, fresh milk, refrigerated meats, ice cream and bread with out bugs, even hot rolls and pies. Now I don't know how the navy reasoned it out, but the officers ate three meals a day while the enlisted ate only two but could pick up coffee and donuts when ever they wished all day long.

The meals were so great that two would have been enough for any one. This cruise was to consume 35 days, including a three day port call in Melbourne, Australia.. It was a beautiful voyage where we enjoyed the ship's pool, sunbathing, movie and played volley-ball with the navy component.

All day when we werent working, yes we had to pull 'O.D.', with the navy guys from the Phillipines manning the guard posts. I noticed that the navy enlisted never saluted us though they did the Navy officers.

When I asked the Navy CPO's why this lack of courtesy? He replied. We didn't know you were officers" and he was correct as we had been wearing our khaki's with no insignia, just as we had done in India. So they were not being disrespectful, they really weren't aware that we were commissioned officers.

Remember how I had criticized the food in Chabua and how I had lost over 35 pounds? Well when we docked in San Francisco just 35 days out of Bombay I had gained 30 pounds during the voyage and when I arrived home nobody believed It as I was almost the same weight as when I left for India.

When we reached Melbourne we all went ashore, except the complement of marines who remained on board. We later learned learned that the Marines were not allowed ashore in Melbourne due to a very bad incident that took place there some time back. It seems a division of Marines was sent to Melbourne, 3,000 of them for some "R. & R." about a year earlier and some one forgot about them and they stayed there for over six months.

With 3,000 Marines roaming the area with nothing to do, some of them met up with a few of those lonely Aussie wives, in fact more than a few. In fact when the Aussie's came home quite a few found their wives pregnant and they had been gone over a year.

This resulted in a number of pitched battles between the Marines and the Aussies and a quick demand by local authorities for the Marines to get off their island. Finally a number of top brass: both U.S. and Australian worked out an agreement that the Marines would depart and neve more return.

We were there three days and found Melbourne to be a great place, good food, lots of sights and the troops said the girls were quite friendly.

The remainder of the voyage to San Francisco was most enjoy and uneventful. Though we had no escort the S.S. Lurline could run between 25 and 30 knots and most subs travel at about 10 knots per hour.

We played a lot of volleyball against the navy crew and there was as Navy captain on board who had been serving with the Air Corps in India for a year and he wasn't too happy with the Navy's attitude towards the Air Corps members on board and told them so. They did have a superior attitude and tried a ruse on us that backfired.

They told us, very confidentially, that there were special ocean currents that performed similarly to the Jet stream in the air. They claimed it was a very fast "river of water" that enabled them to place special containers in it and those containers will get to Hawaii several days sooner than we would. So if we had any mail we would like to get to the States several days sooner, just give them to the Navy and they would take care of them.

What they really intended doing was to have a large party for the crew and passengers on the last night before arriving in Honolulu, and at the party take all of those letters that the gullible Air Corps members wrote and read them aloud.

What they found was many letters proclaiming how great the Navy was in that they could control the ocean currents, and other comments of no matter how great those Navy fellows were that "nothing could really stop the Army Air Corps". They never did read them aloud as they knew we didn't fall for it, thanks to that Navy captain who had served with us in China and liked the Air Corps.

On board the S.S. Lurline with us was a Belgian Priest who had just served as a missionary in China and had done double duty helping the Navy and the Army out as a chaplain. He, was Father Charles Meeus, on his way to the U.S. to visit Bing Crosby who, though it was never publicized, he helped help foreign missionaries by raising money for them.

To do so he would have the missionary give him an outline of what he had done as a missionary and he would write a script about that missionary's toiling in those areas and if he had any photos Bing would have them combined in an article for handouts at the various tours Bing would arrange. Those tours raised many thousand of dollars.

Father Meeus told me while in China he came across one of Gen. Doolittles B-25's that had crashed in China after the raid on Tokyo. On board he found a copy of an old Literary Digest, the forerunner of today's Reader's Digest. he told Bing that the magazine had offered him $25 for it, but Bing said "Don't you dare sell it to them for that, I'll get you a lot more than that and he did, he got him $2,500 for it.

We were almost delirious when we hit San Francisco and we had a great time for a couple days. We did make time for an "ego" trip through China town, wearing our leather jackets with Chinese flags on the back. They really treated us as celebrities and we ate it up, the hams that we were. But my youngest brother was in navigation school near New Orleans, so I hopped a flight to New Orleans and made arrangement to spend two days with him.

As luck would have it I ran intoTom Moyer, who I had met as a cadet when we were at Selman Field in Alabama taking tests to see what we qualified for: be it pilot, bombardier or navigator. Tom went on to pilot training and I to navigation, and now Tom was flying a "nav-trainer" for navigator trainees in those small 3 passenger planes that had 3 navigation compartments: One for map reading; one for deadreckoning and the third for radio navigating.

Tom had a four hour flight scheduled for that day. He said that if I came along I could ride in the co-pilots seat. I readily agreed, as it was a daytime flight and I would be back before my brother would be out of class.

After about two hours flying time, Tom asked for a position report and none of the cadets knew where they were. Fortunately, as they were discussing the situation I glanced out the window and noticed a large roof that said "Edwards, Miss." So I asked them for a chart and located Edwards, Miss. and said this is where we are.

They were perplexed that they had been lost for over an hour and I pinpointed their position in 30 seconds. I never told them about that garage roof as my instructor in flying school always said "Use the best means at your disposal" and I did.

I'll tell you a little tale that instructor told me when I met him in Reykjavik, Iceland where we were both flying the north Atlantic route, I with the Crescent Caravan and he with the airlines. After leaving my brother I caught a flight in to the New Castle Air Base, in Wilmington, Del. where we merely reported in and picked up our 30 day leaves, due after a year in the CBI.

With all that "fruit salad" on our chests: Asiatic theatre & good conduct medals, the CBI patch on our shoulders and first lieutenant's bars on our shoulders we headed home thinking we must look pretty impressive. We felt like we had when we graduated and the sign over the navigation school had read "Through these doors pass the cream of the crop". But some one took issue with that and changed the "o" in crop to be an "a". I guess with all of the adulation we were taking ourselves too seriously. But that didn't last long when you have so many brothers and sisters to set you straight real quick.

I had another "comeuppance" when I ran into the father of one of the members of my football team. The standard uniform caps for officers contain a grommet in them to maintain their shapes. However when flying you had to remove them in order to use head phones and they became a little floppy and looked a little like a taxi cab drivers cap.

I was wearing a trench coat and we never put bars on them. When my friend's father saw me, he warmly greeted me and said "I haven't seen you around for a while, I didn't know you were driving a cab.

It was a little deflating, here I was, the conquering hero having just returned from a year of flying the hump only to be mistaken for a cab driver. I was in for a little more deflation when my fiancee showed me her brother's letter about how the war wouldn't last forever and not to be too hasty about getting married. Remember he was the one I had met in Accra while I was attired in Bermuda shorts & shirt, a pith helmet, Natal boots and a goatee.

Author on left, and his two brothers.

107

That thirty day leave literally flew by and it was back to the work we had been trained for: delivering airplanes and their crews to areas waiting for them so it was back to the New Castle Air Base in Wilmington, Del.

But during that year I had spent in India there had been even newer techniques developed in aerial navigation that we had not be made aware of. So we spent several weeks in the class room learning them while brushing up on the ones we hadn't used on the hump or during our 35 days enroute home or in the 30 day leaves.

My next assignment was to take a C- 46 to Tunisia, in North Africa and again via the southern route: Trinidad, Brazil, Ascension Island, Accra, Casablanca to Tunis. It was a strange crew with "Cal Calloway", a young first lieutenant as the first pilot and Captain Bill Grace, as the co-pilot, both of whom were to be assigned to the Tunis area.

"Cal" was the most loquacious, most self impressed pilot I had ever met. I think he truly believed that he was the greatest pilot that the entire air corps (at that time) had the priviledge of having in it's ranks. He told some of the most outlandish stories you imaginable, one though was possible. He said he had "chandelled" a C-46 which was more common to fighter planes than to cargo types. But I do remember Captain Spurlock when the Jet stream flipped his C-46, he had to do a reverse chandelle to right the air craft. Those ten days with "Cal" seemed more like a year.

After delivering that C-46 to Tunisia I hopped a ride back to Casablanca, then one to Holyhead, Wales, caught the train up to Prestwick, Scotland where there was a C-54

already to go back to the States via Iceland, Newfoundland, New York and then to New Castle.

My next trip was with three other navigators. We took the train to Baer Field in Indiana where we picked up three C-47's for delivery to England via Holyhead, Wales. Once again it was the southern route: Bermuda, Trinidad, Guayana, Belem, Natal, Ascension Islands, Accra, Marrekech,

Casablanca and then a long over water hop up well off the European coast into Wales, where we left the planes and crews.

As I had seen that area several times previously, I headed on up to Prestwick via train. The other three navigators wanted to see the country before heading back and there was no one there to tell them they couldn't.

You learn to fend for yourself after several deliveries and become a rather experience world traveller by making certain that you have the proper curriencies with you be they: south American, African, Italian or English. However most would accept U.S. currency especially in Iceland, Newfoundland, Labrador or Canada. The hardest part was in learning their coins, which could cost you some money if you weren't careful.

One of the rewards of the "Have gun will travel" business was Newfoundland (as was Bermuda) as every article that was rationed in the States was available there and cheaper. So each trip you could make your families and friends quite happy by bringing them many items they needed coupons for at home.

You could get the finest champagne, silks, wools, watches, Canadian Club whiskey, Johnny Walker scotch, butter, etc. and we did not have to go through custom as they never checked the aircraft. The only bad part of that is there was always some one looking to make a fast buck by smuggling in jewelry, watches, etc.

The main offenders were the airline crews as, being paid a lot more than we were, they had the money with which to do it.We called them the "feather merchants" and had little to do with them socially.

We usually were given from 5 days to a week off between trips and I was back home several times a month. So much so that I think a lot of my neighbors though I was a deserter. It was nice though, whether in South American, Africa, Italy, etc. that you would be home again in a few weeks.

One of my most memorable trips was when I took those A-20 medium bombers to Italy in late 1944. There only 2 navigators and we each had 4 planes to be accountable for. This meant that the navigation station in 6 of those planes were empty, it seems that some brain had decided to ship all of the navigatiors via boat to Italy whereas at least six of them could have flown in the their own planes and picked up some valuable experience as we maintained voice contact with each plane in our unit.

All went well until well until we reached Brazil and Shuchuck, who had been one of my instructors in cadet school was senior in rank and flite leader, decided that instead of following the flight plan (that sent us around the coast line) we would cut across the jungles and save time.

Unfortunately when we were only about half way across his plane developed engine trouble and they had to land at a small emergency strip in the jungle for repairs.

Unfortunately, that strip was too short for an A-20 to take off from and it would have to be disassembled and trucked out.

So he radioed me to take his 3 aircraft as part of my unit until we reached Recife, Brazil. Upon arriving at Recife I was informed by the operation's officer that I now had a flight of seven planes to take to Italy.

This made my pilot, an old guy of 24, nicknamed "Pop" Wilson. the flight leader. I was a little older than "Pop" and we were both first lieutenants so, I guess because I had a CBI patch on my uniform and it made me look more experienced, so he (Pop Wilson) said he would leave all of flying instructions to me. Those A- 20's had two serious drawbacks, so far as a navigator was concerned.

First, they had no automatic pilot which meant that the pilot had to hand fly it all the way across the ocean and hand flying does not hold an exact heading. In other words the pilot could stray off course, on either side and you had no way of knowing it.

Secondly, there was no ADF, or automatic direction finder, whose needle would point to, when approaching a station, or back to, if you passed it. the station. Why was that important?

113

Well, we were over water heading for a little island only 8 miles long and 3 miles wide, over 1,000 miles away from any other land. If by any chance we were in bad weather, or at night, we could pass over it and keep flying until we ran out of fuel and have ditch in the ocean.

Since this was a daylight flight we could not utilize the stars, as they weren't out. The only thing available was the sun which gives us a single line of position, goes went completely around the world, that we would be on, but exactly where only heaven (not a pun) knows.

So if we overflew Ascension, as a friend of mine had, the chances of being found were about one in a thousand, as my friend evidently discovered as they never found his plane or his crew.

Luckily, and I truly mean luckily, everything went perfectly as per flight plan. My pilot did an excellent job of holding headings and we hit Ascension right on our E.T.A. or estimated time of arrival.

One thing that was amazing was the way those other six pilots flew that ocean. When the weather was clear they were all over that sky, but when it began to cloud up or rain heavily, they would stick so close to "Magellan" than I had one right wing tip almost in my nose position and a left one on the other side.

The navigator rode in the nose of the A-20 and held a board on his lap with his charts on it. He wore his parachute at all times to which was attached a one man rubber life raft and he sat on it for the whole flight. In that life raft were several items but one of them we found out years later was just something to make is feel safe. It was a container of yellow dye that we were to put in the water in case of sharks and "repel" them. But as we were later to find out that the sharks didn't know they were afraid of it.

The runway at Ascension was 6,000 feet long of which the first 2,000 feet were uphill, the second was level and the third was down hill. This was because the island was of solid rock and that was the best they could do, but better than no island at all.

Upon landing I met a First Lieutenant who looked familiar and when I asked him his name I found he was the brother of my old parish priest back home.They had some very pretty beaches, a fair officers club and outdoor movies. So when I asked if they would like to take a couple of days "R & R" to which they all readily agreed, so I spent 3 days there visiting with my friend.

From there we headed for Roberts field in Liberia, amid the rubber plantations and then to Marrekech and Casablanca, Oran, Sicily, Naples and Rome. I knew my brother John was a pilot of a B-24 in Italy, whose group which, when we landed in Naples I learned was in Cerignola When I checked about how I could visit him. all of the crews wanted to come along, so I went to Cerignola with all seven planes.

Needless to say we caused a little commotion when seven A-20 medium bombers flew into a B-24 heavy bomber base, but they were very friendly and solicitous They told me that my brother was out on a bombing mission and gave me his tail numbers. Fortunately they had given me the wrong numbers as the one they gave to me never returned from that mission, but my brother's plane did.

After visiting several hours, the base was anxious to get those 7 planes out of their parking areas, so we took off and returned to Rome. We landed at Capaducina airbase which is an experience in itself as it is all up hill. so you have to either land uphill or downhill depending upon the wind direction. But taking off up hill is a little disconcerting as the whole time you are gaining altitude on take off, the airstrip is still the same distance below you until you are finally beyond it and really airborne.

The next day we delivered the planes and the crews to a base just outside of Rome and when I checked with base ops to see if I could catch a flight to Casablanca where I could catch a flight to Wales or Scotland I received a little shock.

The group commander, a full colonel, informed me that I was to remain as his navigation officer, but not to worry as he would see that I got Captains bars shortly. I asked how that was possible as I was on detached service and I didn't see how he could promote me even if he wanted to.

However I did remain and made several bombing missions with them, hitting marshalling yards, in Italy, full of freight trains. Several days later the Colonel admitted he had no authority to keep me and I could start back home.

I managed to catch a ride into Casablanca and subsequently a hop to Holyhead, Wales, then by train Prestwick where I caught a C-54 home via Reyjavik, Stephensville and on into New York. But while in Reyjavik I met two former people from my past: Gen Casey Vincent from the 14th. A.F. in Kunming and Bill Miller, a brother of a high school classmate and himself a navigator with the airlines.

Upon checking into the Degink Hotel (base boq) I made a wrong turn and went into the wrong room. It was Gen. Casey Vincent's room who, immediately upon seeing my CBI patch he got up and said, "Ah, one of my boys from the hump, welcome to Iceland". That evening he bought me a drink and that was one of the few times in my career a general ever bought me a drink.

As to Bill Miller, when I told him I was recently at Roberts Field, in Liberia, he said "I hope you gave Katie a call while you were there". His sister Katie and I had been class mates in both grade and school, but I did not know she was married to the owner of a rubber plantation in Liberia upon which the airstrip was built.

Later that evening I met another Pan Am navigator, he was Doug McLeod, one of my instructors at the Miami University's school of navigation (run by Pan Am) and he told me a story I never forgot. He said, "Andy, You met my wife (when you were a cadet) but we have since divorced, the reason being that we had no children and each of us blamed the other. So I remarried and about 11 months l later my new wife gave birth to a baby boy, so I, facetiously, sent a christmas card to my X enclosing a picture of my son".

He said it was about 7 months later that he received a letter from his "ex" and in it was a photo of a baby girl along with the comment "attached is photo of my daughter <u>and I know that I am the mother</u>".

Doug had a wonderful sense of humor and was extremely proud of being Scottish. So much so that when one cadet said "Mr. McLeod, are you Scotch". He answered, "Scotch is a drink of liquor I am a Scot and the next cadet who gets that wrong will flunk this course".

He was heading east into London, while I was enroute to the States and knew that eventually we'd meet again along the way. But there was nothing more boring than "dead heading" as it was like a bus man's holiday just looking out of the windows into the darkness at night or at the wide expanses of ocean during the day time.

I never liked to fly unless there was a need for it and was the navigator having something to occupy my time. Of course it was always an experience for our passengers as they were either heading overseas for the first time or better yet on their way home after a tour of duty.

After departing Reyjavik we next landed at Harmon Field in Newfoundland where we ate and did some fast shopping while the plane was being refueled, necessary maintenance being done, a new crew taking over, etc.

I alway liked Harmon Field as the weather was usually brisk and clean, the food was always good and they had so many items of food and clothing that were rationed in the state that we could pick up and at lower prices.

Several hours after departing Harmon we were landing at Mitchell Field in Long Island where the passengers and cargo were unloaded and checked by customs. Customs didn't concern itself with us and we would immediately depart for good old New Castle Air Base in Wilmingon, Del.

After checking in at operation's office I would take my logs and charts to the navigation office otherwise the records would never log if, or were I went. Years later I found that I should have been a little more thorough as some on my trips never made it into the base files and it badly affected the total of hours I had actually flown versus those on record.

If it were night time we would head for the Officers club for a nightcap and then hit the sack. We would normally have four to six days off between trips and told when you were next scheduled out and as I said if it night time you hit the sack for an early rising to head on home. But if it were daylight I would hop into my car and head off for Pittsburgh just six hours away.

I had been quite fortunate that a fellow navigator sold me his car when he was sent overseas on a permanent assignment. It sure was a life saver as it saved me so much time that would have been normally wasted by having to catch a ride into Philadelphia and then catching a train to downtown Pittsburgh where some one had to pick me up.

After a pleasant week at home with family and friends it was back to "grind", but this time there was something in the air when I reported in to the chief navigators office. Up til now I had delivered a C-87 to India, spent a year flying the Hump, had delivered four C-47's to England, a C-46 to Tunisia and seven A-20's to Italy. I could sense a change in the atmosphere, something was new and different as all of the old scuttlebut we had heard about the Air Corps starting it's own airline was now coming true.

The major in charge of scheduling navigators called us all into a special meeting and said he had been requested by the group commander to forward him (the C.O.) a list of 33 navigators for specialized training to coordinate each and all to the exact same routine of reporting positions, flight data,weather, etc., for use in a whole new venture.

They were establishing regular flights to europe via pre-selected bases and routes with bases in Newfoundland, Iceland, the Azores, England and Cairo and Casablanca in north Africa, with Bermuda as an alternate when strong winds were encountered between Newfoundland and the Azores.

There were to be 12 flights daily out New Castle Air Base (Wilmington, Del) into Mitchell Field (Long Island), then into Harmon Field (Newfoundland), then Reyjavik, (Iceland) and Heathrow, (London) or to North Africa via the Azores.

The crews would R.O.N. (remain over night) at those bases and the planes continue on with new crews. Your route was determined by the flight number your plane was assigned when it left Mitchell Field. If your plane began as flight # 542 to Casablanca then, after RONing you would crew flight #542 every day enroute to and return, ditto for flights to England and later to Paris.

The cargo: be it troops, mail, special supplies, diplomats, U.S.O. troupes, etc. would board at Mitchell Field, Long Island after we flew the plane in from NCAB (New Castle Air Base). On the return flight everything (and everybody) was offloaded at Mitchell, after which we returned to NCAB.

To reach the goal of 12 flights departing every day depended upon the availability of sufficient C-54's, which was almost an impossible task. Even with the planes only stopping at each base long enough to refuel, giving the passengers a short time to eat, as the plane was checked for any enroute maintenance that arose, it still averages three days for the plane to make the round trip. This necessitated a bare minimum of 36 plane with 12 departing every day, leaving no planes as standby to fill in if an emergency arose.

I never knew how many we originally started with but we did start with 33 crews, so I guess we were operating with less than 11 flights per day. That would have required crews for each flight R.O.N.ing in

Newfoundland, Iceland, Azores, England, Casablanca, Cairo and at least one, stand- by, crew in Bermuda. This would require at least 60 crews to maintain those 12 flights a day and we only had 33 full crews. I know as I was one of the 33 navigators selected to fly on the "Crescent Caravan" to Europe on a daily round rip service. It was so named as it's flight path was in the form of a crescent, but eventually it would be come the military transportation service or better know as 'MATS".

It took the crews an average of six days to make the round trip. This meant we were flying three round trips each month or about thirty six a year as they gave us about four days off after each trip. This was less than the five days they gave us for ferry missions, but we were usually gone longer on them.

As best as I can recall we started in mid 1944 and a year later we shifted our base of operations from New Castle to Westover Field in Massachussetts, shortly after Paris had been recaptured and soon became out main terminus, to and from Europe. As such. the demands on our operations were greatly increased.

In fact the Navy also got in the act with one flight a day, also a C-54 as we used. They (Navy) flew only one flight per day into Paris and I vividly remember that while we were flying cargo, mail, troops, etc., they were flying in furniture and supplies for their officer's club for over two weeks.

When I asked a navy commander why the Navy took care of the officer's club first, he replied, "When our men are comfortable they perform better so we want them to be comfortable, maybe he was right but I thought the war had first priority.

Daily flying the ocean becomes routine and some times very boring due to the type of personnel and cargo we normally carried.

There were days that were anything but boring, such as when transporting the worst casualities from the "battle of the bulge",or carrying high ranking diplomats from Paris to New York enroute to a United Nations

Conference in San Francisco, U.S.O. troupes, flying through hurricanes, long hours of bad weather when you couldn't pinpoint your position, etc.

After a year of flying the hump, over another year of ferrying planes around the globe and close to seventy roundtrips between New York and Europe, etc., I felt it time to start devoting more time to my wife and family back home. It had been quite glamorous for a while hiring out my sextant.

I knew I owed my country an awful lot for giving me both the education and opportunity to serve in the capacity I had, but now the war was finally over. So I put in for a discharge but was turned down due to my celestial navigation skills and my experience in over water flying.

I felt that there were many other navigator with the same skills just waiting for the same experiences I had. As in every form of life, politics plays a role and my oldest brother, very politically involved in the state of Pennsylvania made a few calls and I was finally able to hang up that "have sextant will travel" sign and put away that sextant with about 4,000 flying hours that included "ferrying" those plane, flying the hump from India to China and over 70 round trips across the north Atlantic ocean.

The following is a variation on an old poem that was written by a fellow humpster. It sums it up quite well as at times it seems "we really did serve our hitch in hell".

"HITCH IN HELL"

(The lament of a hump pilot)

"By Bill Wise, one of them"
I'm sitting here a thinking

of the things I left behind.

I hate to put on paper

what is running through my mind.

I've flown so many missions,

cleared for hundreds of miles around.

Andrew Kelly

A rougher place this side of hell,

　I'm sure cannot be found.

But there's a certain consolation,

　so listen while I tell,

When we die we'll go to heaven,

　cuz "we did our hitch in hell"

We've flown so many drums of gas,

　Chennault should rule the land.

We've checked a million mags,

　I guess and cleared them all by hand.

We've been airborne on a Chinese flight

　in weather thick as ink.

We've fought the thundertorms at night

　and ice enough to build a rink

So when our work on earth s done,

    our friends behind will tell:

These boys all went to heaven,'

    cause they did their hitch in hell.

We take our Atabrine, those bitter little pills,

    to buildup resistance to fever, aches and chills.

We've seen a zillion Zeroes

    zoom above us in the sky.

As we run like hell for cover

    when those yellow bastards fly.

Put out those lights and cigarettes,

    we're force to tell the crew.

This isn't any picnic,

    it's another hitch in Hell,

And when the final taps are sounded,

    and we've shed our earthly cares.

We'll put on our best wing parade

    upon those golden stairs.

And when those Angels greet us,

    their harps they'll gladly play.

We'll draw a million beer rations,

    and drink them in a day.

We'll hear old Gabriel blow his horn,

    and St. Peter loudly yell:

Front seats for the boys of the C.B.I., for

    They've done their hitch in Hell"

I'll always have fond memories of my years in the military, of the places I've seen,the fantastic trips we took but mainly of the extraordinary people I was able to associate with who did their jobs willingly so that we could do ours.

The media seems to equate the military mainly with officers, but having been both a staff sergeant as well as an officer, I can tell you it has long been the roll of enlisted ranks,(be they:Air Force Army, Marines or the navy), to be the force that won or lost the battle, the campaign, to keep the planes in the sky, to enable the Magellans, like myself, to get to their destinations. Thank God for them, for they have been and still are, the backbone of all the Services.

Since retiring I have been fortunate to be a member of many retiree military associations and to have served on their boards in one capacity or other: the Air Force Association (four times as president), the Retired Officers Association, the Retired Enlisted Association, Air Force Sergeant's Association, the Retired

Enlisted Association, the China, Burma, India, the D.R. Ahead, (retired navigator's), Hump Pilots Association, Retired Officers Activities (R.A.O) at Fairchild Air Base and I am still the Commander of the C.B.I. veterans Basha here in Spokane.

One organization that I am very proud to have been associated with for many years as a docent, is Fairchild Air Force Base's Heritage Museum, where my A-2 flight jacket (with the Chinese flag on the back) is displayed in one of their display cases.

One of our other docents, Major Jerry Kolstee, wanted to give it's presence a little special attention. He asked me of all the places I wore it in the service. He then compiled a notice to place below the jacket. He entitled it "That Old A-2 Jacket With The Chinese Flag On The Back!

I guess this notice sums up the many areas it has visited since I originally "Hired out my sextant"to the old Army Air Corps'

Although it was in a featured display cabinet, it had not a word as to why it was there. So to the casual observer it was just an old A-2 jacket hanging in the Fairchild Air Force Base Museum, but unlike others, it had an old Army Air Corps Ferry (transport) Command patch on it's front, a C.B.I. patch on the left arm and a Chinese Flag on the back.

"Though it was evidently here because of it's history, what would that history be if it were able to speak? So let us imagine what it might just tell us, if it could.

It was issued at Rosekranz Field, St. Joseph, Mo. in December of 1942, to a very green second lieutenant, and it made quite a few excursions and detours before it landed at the Fairchild Heritage Museum in 1985. It had been to every continent in the world and practically every nation on those continents.

It flew *"the Hump"* from India into China for the year of 1943, was worn by the navigator who found the famous correspondent Eric Sevareid and 19 others, who had bailed out of a disabled C-46 transport plane and alit in an 8,000 foot deep ravine in the jungles of Burma.

It was worn while delivering 7 A-20 medium bombers to Italy, a C-46 to Tunisia, 4 C-47's to Wales, in 1944, a C-87 (B-24 cargo version) to India in 1943. It has flown the from New York City to Paris, London, Casa Blanca, Cairo, etc. over 70 times.

It had met such old figures as: Generalissimo Chiang Kai Chek, General Claire Chennault (Flying Tigers) Gen. "Vinegar Joe" Stillwell, General Casey Vincent (youngest general in the Air Corps at age 29), Lord Louis Mountbatten and many national and international diplomats, USO Troops, etc.

It survived the jungles of South America, Burma, and India, flew over the Alps, the Himalaya's, the Tropics, the Arctic, Nepal, the Amazon River, the Eiffel Tower in Paris, visited the Taj Mahal in India, the Vatican, London's Big Ben, the Rock of Gibralter, the North Pole, the Pyramids, Mount Everest, and many others I have forgotten.

You might say "It's been around"..I know, as I was in it every place it went". It's still attracting lots of attention as it is in a special case in the Fairchild Air Force Museum.

We never stopped to realize that the vast majority of troops in all of the service were either in their late teens or their early twenties. It never occurred to me until I took those seven A-20's to Italy and the commander of the flight of Lt Wilson asked me if I would assume command as I was more familiar of what we would encounter enroute.So I did so, brought it to mind was that. although he was only twenty four years old, all of the crews called him "Pop" Wilson.

I only hope that if our present day teenagers are called to duty as in world war -11 that they will also mature as rapidly as did the ones back then.

Since the end of WW-11 There has arisen many very strange reports concerning the region of the Atlantic Ocean between the coast of Florida out to the island of Bermuda.

There were many strange disappearances from single aircraft up formations of five or six planes from the Naval squadrons based in Florida.

What was quite puzzling to me is that while in cadet school at the University of Miami, while studying celestial navigation all of our flight training was mainly in that same area and we never experienced any abnormalities, nor did any class in the five or six years the school was in operation from 1940 til 1946.

What is most puzzling is that we were flying cargo type airplanes with no type of armaments while all the ones that disappeared were fully armed with the latest in aircraft armament. Why were we, of the unarmed variety untouched while the one's capable of defending themselves were the ones victimized. Most puzzling aspect was that, til date, no one has ever found any reason for those disappearances.

Some of those, including a plane with many passengers disappeared not very far from the coast of Florida, possibly within sight of it.

There were all kinds of theories from men from outer space to some powers, also from there, that absorbed all of the aircrafts' electrical power making them inoperable and causing them to crash with no radio capacity to contact or inform of their problems or to seek help, but todate there have been no answers as to why we flew all through that area with no problems while so many others became tragic victims?

All things included: the good, the bad and inbetween know I'll always have fond memories of all my years in the military, of the many places I've seen, the fantastic trips we took but mainly because of the many extraordinary people I was priviledged to associated with. People who did their jobs so willingly so that we could do ours.

The media seems to associate the military mainly with officers, but having been both a staff sergeant as well as an officer, I can tell you that there were many enlisted men for whom I had greater respect than I had for a number of self impressed officers. While in most cases, though it's an officer who gives the orders, those orders would not be worth a hill of beans if it weren't for the sergeants and their men who implemented those orders, many times at the risk of their lives.

Since the inception if the military, it's long been the role of the enlisted ranks, be they the Air Force, Army, Marines, or the Navy, to be the weapons that win or lose the battle, the campaign or kept those planes in the sky and to enable that Magellan, like myself, to reach their destinations, thank God for them, for they are backbones of all of the services.

Yet, when I view the hours of training we underwent, the thousands and thousands of persons who were involved in teaching, learning, in flying the millions of hours in the in the air, the millions of miles, of the billions of dollars spent in new equipment, the new theories, the installation and servicing of it, the new careers created I never imagined that some day, in our lifetime that we would become obsolete.

That raises interesting an interesting problem? Were we really pioneers of an industry or mere guinea pigs of a drastically needed skill that further technology would soon render as now passe?

However, no matter how much they change the technology or the methods of travel to those foreign lands they cannot change my memories of those memorable places we did visit, those memorable sights such as the Taj Mahal, in India, the Eiffel Tower and the Notre Dame Cathedral, in Paris, the Coliseum, in Italy, Big Ben, in London, the Nile river and the Pyramids, in Egypt, Mount Everest and that member of the seven wonders of the world: that narrow guaged switch back railroad up to Darjeeling in Nepal, the beautiful islands of the Azores, the Rock of Gibralter. the Alps, in Switzerland and all of the beautiful sights of the South Pacific, Alaska and others.

So when I really look back, I hope every and all of guinea pigs of the future get to enjoy it as much as I did.

Pioneers or Guinea Pigs.

Apparently, there is little, if any, distinction between being a pioneer in a large scale project or merely a guinea pig, especially when that project involved traveling through the celestial skies.

Prior to WW1, little thought had been given to flight, until those innovative gas balloons (Civil War inspired) were used by artillery post spotters during that War. Those balloons, tethered high above enemy lines, enabled observors to direct artillery fire upon enemy positions.

Even then, air travel wasn't envisioned when those balloons were first created. Yet there were dreamers who saw them as possible weapons of war or even transportation. Two of them, Orville and Wilbur Wright, developed a heavier than air craft that success-fully became airborne and would revolutionize both future warfare and world air travel.

Barely into my twenties, I was given the opportunity to participate in a large scale military project that would greatly impact the war effort, and eventually global travel.

Prior to WW-II, there was comparatively little international air travel as, though the aircraft were capable of flying long distances over water or untracked lands, the air crews had little knowledge, or means, of plotting courses over tractless expanses of water, of being able to ascertain their positions in the sky along the flight path to distant nations. Surface transportation, (ships) had a workable, method of determining their position on those waters, via the stars and planets.

It was called "celestial" navigation, via which the stars, sun, moon and planets could enable the ship's navigator to establish and maintain a path upon those rough seas in relation to the positions of those celestial bodies in the skies. Yet, till then, the instrument used to determine those positions, was not adaptable for use in aircraft.

There was one, comparatively small, (compared to today,) airline that experimented with, and developed, a method to adapt that instrument, for such use. That airline, Pan American Airways flew aircraft with fuselages in the shape of streamlined boats and called Clipper ships (or "flying boats") that were capable of taking off from or landing upon the surfaces of large bodies of water.

That instrument, known as a sextant, was eventually adapted for usage in large aircraft as Army officials, via negotiations with the Pan American Airways, (and it's top navigator Charlie Lunn) established a school of celestial navigation at the University of Miami, Fla. to teach the art of celestial navigation to military personnel.

With Hitler running amok in Europe the USA was rapidly being drawn into war, it was imperative that the U.S. be able to utilize large aircraft (then on the drawing boards) to transport needed supplies, vital materials and personnel to Europe and other points of the world as quickly as possible so those navigators were needed yesterday. At that period of time we, members of the 639th tank destroyer battalian (29th Field Artillery Div.)

were on maneuvers in the Carolina's (when Japan attacked Pearl Harbor on December 7th, 1941). We were immediately returned to our home bases to await new orders and be given opportunities to apply for flight training.

There we, who had successfully completed those very grueling tests by the Army Air Corps, were assigned to train in the various flying categories. We qualified for; bombardiers, navigators or for pilot training. I, for navigational training, was sent to Pan American's school at the University of Miami.

Question? Would this training making us pioneers in this field or merely guinea pigs in a large scale experiment? And what of the passengers, we'd transport to all areas of the globe, would they too, be "pioneers of air travel", or merely lowly guinea pigs, as we struggled to become experienced "celestial navigators"?

Upon completion of that very rigorous Pan American course (and transitional training at Robideaux Field in "St. Joe" Mo. I was assigned to the New Castle Air Base in

Wilmington, Del. for duty. Shortly after arriving there I was flown to St. Paul, Mn., as part of a crew, to pick up a C-87 (B-24 cargo version) to deliver to Chabua, in the province of Assam, India, half way around the world, via of Nashville, Tenn. to onload 19 passengers & cargo and head to the CBI theatre, 13,000 miles away.

The pilots: Captain's Ed Fallon, of Boston and Ed Akerman from Gadsen, Alabama, were among the best I would ever fly with. The next day we departed for Morrison Field in Palm Beach, Fla. and on to Puerto Rico and points south, enroute to India via: South America, Central and north Africa, Egypt, Arabia, Kurachi, New Delhi and Agra in India and our final stop Chabua, in that province of Assam on the Bramaputra river on the western Burmese border.

Chabua's air base's buildings were of bamboo structure with thatched roofs, dirt floors and embedded into a large tea plantation (infested with snakes and wild animals) with a single air strip. It was the gateway into (and exit out of) China, for every plane, item and person heading there: Diplomats, envoys, military personnel (enlisted and brass), foreign correspondents, material, weapons, personnel, aircraft, etc.

But that's putting the cart before the horse as, though we arrived safely, I had discovered a vast difference between flight training missions vs actually assuming responsibility for the delivery of an expensive aircraft loaded with valuable cargo and well trained members of the military to a remote corner of the earth over many strange lands, seas, jungles and deserts.

Prior til then, I had taken the theory of celestial navigation, the long months of training, etc., for granted. Now I questioned every action I took, for there was no instructor looking over my shoulder. just passengers and crew looking to me to get them to their destinations safely! There was no room for second guessing.

We departed Morrison Field in Palm Beach, Florida on a daylight flight to Puerto Rico, with little wind to concern me, either at take off or at flight level. Nor any worry about variation (magnetic attraction) as it is at just only one or two degrees in that area. Enroute there were many islands to use as check points, so we flew practically via the flight plan with no wind or variation to affect the compass headings.

The second day's journey to the island of Trinidad, was all over water, and mainly via dead reckoning and the flight plan. Being a daylight flight there was no chance to utilize any celestial navigation as the sun provides a single line of position, only if you can catch it directly overhead at noon time when it will give you a definite position, but we did have "ADF"(automatic direction finder) that would point towards destination when within 200 miles.

It gave me the opportunity of using the driftmeter to establish drift and ground speed via timing the white caps. It was all we needed as the weather was very calm few little winds to affect us and we arrived in Port of Spain exactly on schedule,

Next morning, while awaiting tower instructions for take off position and awaiting our turn, a P-39 taxied too close to our right wing tip. Needless to say his prop slashed our wing tip making us inoperative for flying that day. Our crew chief was quite concerned that our wing tanks might catch fire, so he made a very hurried inspection to assure us that all was well.

We taxied back to our parking spot where the ground crew assessed the damaged. It would require a new wing tip that would have to be flown in from the States and it would involve a week to ten day layover.

We spent a very pleasant, and uneventful ten days in which we were able to really tour the island and towns on foot, by car and by even small planes before taking off for Waller Field in George-town, British Guayana, a remote setting completely ringed by jungle type land and presented no problems. We were in and out very quickly on the next day's leg into Belem, in the mouth of the Amazon river, again overland with no problems.

The leg into Recife (Brazil) and on to the little island of Natal, 100 miles east of Recife, to top off our fuel tanks, would be the final leg prior to the main challenge.

This would be my baptism, my first big test involving the use of celestial navigation, the strong point of our training by Pan American Air ways at the University of Miami. Now I'd find how much of those very detailed instructions I had absorbed, yes, this would be my baptism into celestial navigation and hopefully elevate me from Guinea pig status to that of a Pioneer.

The flight, a night flight, would depart Natal shortly after 20:00 local time and should arrive in Accra at day-break, if all went well! Fortunately on that long flight the weather cooperated beautifully.

With cloudless skies, the stars were easy to identify, the air craft was very steady, it was a joy to use the sextant and I found that nebulous, elusive factor called confidence. I knew I had arrived as a navigator as we hit Accra right on the nose, both on-time and course and my eta wasn't a minute off.

Accra, on the Gold Coast of Africa, had an extremely large native, outdoor, market place and though it's atmosphere may have been appreciated by the local natives, it's aroma was so pronounced, that we could actually smell it at flight altitude upon our arrival. On subsequent trips through there, I found it to be true the year round.

The next legs into Khartoum, Egypt; Aden, Arabia; then on into Kurachi, India and finally Chabua went like clockwork. Now confidence is a strange, badly needed, trait that affects each of us differently, and during the entire flight I had been very concerned with the crew's confidence in me. They hadn't requested me to be their Magellan as I was assigned to them by group headquarters at the New Castle Air Base.

They had no way of knowing that they too, were to be guinea pigs, of my first overseas venture and naturally I was very concerned on every leg as to their confidence in my abilities, (and my own in myself).

It was several weeks following our arrival in Chabua that I found they'd been more concerned about my opinion of them, as it was also their first voyage overseas, and they had assumed I was an old hand at it. They said "We weren't worried about you as you had that look of knowing what you were doing and we wondered what you thought about us".

That served me in good stead later, when as a charter member of the Crescent Caravan, and flying regular round trip routes between New York and London: Paris, Casa Blanca, Cairo, etc., especially when flying in inclimate weather with no stars visable. You learned to relax knowing that, sooner or later, a star was going to appear but, even if it didn't, at times you had loran and always deadreckoning to work with.

Yes we, the crews and passengers alike, were "both pioneers and guinea pigs" in establishing celestial navigation in the quest of inaugurating air travel over vast expanses of oceans. Now, not even the crews were aware that, they too, were "volunteers" in this new concept. Many assumed it to be an old concept and we were merely the latest models.

After the Hump, prior to joining the Crescent Caravan (fore runner of MATS), we, the early graduates of Pan Am's Navigation School, were assigned to ferry many bombers and transports over seas to Africa, Europe, British Isles, Egypt, India and China.

It was very similar to the old westerns that Richard Boone had created in his Paladin series, except his motto was "have gun -will travel" while ours was "have sextant - will travel" as we augmented the combat crews assigned to those aircraft to deliver them to their destinations and then find our way home.

The Army Air Corps, apparently, hadn't much confidence in it's army trained navigators assigned to those combat crews and I felt they handled it quite badly, for they shipped them over seas via ships and did not give them the chance to fly with us for the experience.

This was particularly noticeable when Lt. Shuchuck (who had been one of my instructors in navigation school) and I were each assigned four A-20 medium bombers for delivery to Italy in mid 1944 as all 8 of those A-20 crews navigators were sent by surface vessels.

At least six of them could have ridden along in the vacant navigators compartments for the experience. I eventually delivered seven of those planes to a little base outside of Rome, Italy due to Shuchuck's plane making an emergency landing at a little strip in the jungles of Brazil, The strip was too short for an A-20 to take off from and it, later, had to be disassembled and trucked out. So the other three planes from his flight were assigned to me to complete their journey.

There was another memorable incident on that trip as the C.O. of the base, in Italy, who accepting those planes said "Lieutenant Kelly, we are short of navigators here so I'm keeping you, but do not worry I will guarantee you very quick promotions while here".

Although I reminded him I was on detached service, and he couldn't promote me, he still had me fly several missions (raiding marshalling yards in northern Italy) with his group. Several days later he said that I was correct and I could go back to the States and bring him some more airplanes.

A most perplexing aspect to each trip was, after delivering the planes, was having to seek transportation back to the States and that often presented challenges as many of those bases were in remote areas with little access to other bases.

We had to hitch rides from base to base until reaching Prestwick, Scotland to catch rides to the States via Rekjavik, Iceland, Stephensville, Newfoundland and either Goose Bay, Labrador or Moncton, Canada then on into Mitchell Field, N.Y. and eventually to home base at New Castle Air Base in Wilmington, Delaware.

Fortunately I never lost any of my travel orders but I did run into many unusual situations where I learned how to cope with the various shapes and forms of transportation as well as living quarters. One thing you had to learn was to carry currency from the various areas that you felt you may be travelling through in case there were no military bases nearby. That foreign money created a custom for us, called the "Short Snorter". More on this later.

It was fairly simple finding transportation back to the States after delivering planes to England, but landing in Italy, Tunisia, etc., it wasn't alway that easy. Fortunately for us the educational systems in Europe, north Africa, etc. are much more productive, than in the States, as every where you went: be it Casa Blanca, Tunis, Paris, Rome, Khartoum, Kurachi or Calcutta you had little trouble conversing with shop owners, travel agents, taxi cabs, etc. as they could speak several languages but mainly they all spoke English.

That certainly helped in getting from city to city and from country to country and eventually back home and it made your "Short Snorter" more impressive. The short snorter originated when members of the old "Ferry Command", later the "Air Transport Command" wanted mementoes of each country they visited.

They found that they could use their currency to do so and it took very little space in your wallet. You used a piece of currency from each country you visited, had some one: local, crew member or friend sign it, date it and taped it to the one from the last country you visited and you ended up with a very long (in our cases) strings of foreign currencies all taped to U.S. dollar bills. My first one began in Puerto Rico, was added to in Trinidad, British Guayana, Brazil, the various African, Egyptian, Arabian, Indian and Chinese currencies. I later had some over 45 bills long, that I gave to various members of my family as mementoes.

Serving as guinea pigs to prove other peoples theories, in this case aerial celestial navigation, certainly paid dividends to me, and those other pioneers of the Pan American Airways School of Navigation, for we not only aided the nation's (and the free world's war efforts) it gave us immense pride in our accomplishments: travel beyond our wildest dreams, experiences we could never have imagined and careers that people would pay millions to have, most of all, the confidence it created in us and pride in those accomplishments.

I can recall instances on dark cloudy nights that I didn't have all of that confidence, when I couldn't see a star, and we were too far out over the ocean for effective radio, A.D.F. or loran transmission and turbulence was too strong to expect usable results from dead reckoning - so - you appeared busy and confident for the benefit of your crew and passengers.

No, I never met any of those unnamed persons, whose theories we were priviledged to prove, but without them the world would be decidedly different, but I sincerely thank God for them.

Imagine the pride in being able to board any airplane (that was equipped with the proper instruments of course) knowing you can guide it to any spot on the globe! No, I never met any of those talented deep thinkers, but I thank the Good Lord for that chance to be one of their guinea pigs and later a pioneer.

In retrospect, I wonder how WW-II would have ended if all the equipment and personnel delivered to England, Europe, Africa, Asia and the far east, via air, had not been delivered as quickly as they were, due to the theories of those dedicated few being so accurate?

There were several million young men (and women) involved in the creation of the Air Transport Command (originally the Ferry Command) that made delivery of both personnel and material a reality. If the confidence, and opportunities, given me was also given them, then millions of lives benefitted greatly from being a part of that program.

That confidence was to carry over into civilian life as it gave me the motivation to apply for positions in the business world, that I would never have considered, having completed only two years of high school prior to entering the service.

Those application blanks and resumes only listed me as a veteran who had reached the rank of colonel and no one ever questioned my education. I was able to attend many industry technical schools in: H.V.A.C. and Hydronic products, their sales features. installation procedures, trouble shooting, service and management schools, plus seminars in hydronic heating and aircondition fields that, that I would not have qualified for, educational-wise. Another plus was that you were not awed by titles. After having met so many heads of state, high ranking military, diplomats-correspondents, etc. and speaking to them at their level.

What office manager, or corporation executive was going to make you ill at ease after viewing your resume of meeting such world famous individuals as: Gen. Chiang Kai Chek, Lord Louis Mountbatten; Generals: such as Claire Chennault,"Vinegar" Joe Stillwell; Casey Vincent, Chief Justice Wm.

O. Douglas, Correspondents such as Eric Sevareid and Charles W. Vandercook, movie stars like Betty Hutton and Van Heflin, etc., etc.

What daily business tasks could tax your ingenuity more so than daily flights to Paris, Casablanca, Kunming, Kurachi, Cairo, London, Bombay, etc.? You learned to cope with challenges, large or small, fully confident that you were capable of handling them.

My football coach at Duquesne Prep school had given us the trite expressions such as "your opponents are no different from you in that "they put their uniforms on one leg at a time". You soon found that world and military leaders did the same, as did business leaders and they didn't awe you.

In fact, in many instances, you "awed the business brass" via Your rank, the many foreign countries you had visited, or served in; the many times you had transversed the globe and it's oceans, the famous persons you had met. You soon learned that a low key approach was much more effective than trying to impress others and to let them try "to impress you" after reading your resume.

I often wondered later, when I was serving as chairman of the board of trustees at a large University, what the reaction of the University's president (and it's many knowledgeable professors) would have been, had they known that their boss (so to speak) had but two years of high school education under his belt?

But there, as in the business world, once you had analyzed the situation, you recognized that any university, large or small, consists of two factors: Those possessing the expertise and students who desired that expertise.

Everything else is merely back-ground support to enable those possessors of that expertise (the professors) to teach and impart that knowledge to those who desire it, (the students). All else is merely the setting in which to transfer that expertise (knowledge) to the students who need it.

Those military leaders, who faced the almost impossible task of delivering those vital supplies, aircraft and personnel, had no way of knowing how much they would positively affect the future of the U.S.A. (and world travel) so beneficially, by instilling so much confidence into those who served our nation during those times of stress.

Not only did they find the solutions to teach us the skills of celestial navigation, and/or piloting) to deliver aircraft, supplies and personnel to distant spots of the globe, they showed us, the crews of those aircraft, that we were capable of undertaking, seemingly impossible, tasks and over-coming the many obstacles of life, that we would not have even thought of challenging, prior to then..

Celestial navigation enabled us to use the celestial bodies as highway signs on the paths to foreign lands. So whether guinea pigs or pioneers, we were well rewarded for our endeavors, those of us who survived, that is! The ones who didn't survive were the real heroes.

As a high school drop out, I had never envisioned that some day I would guide a C-

87 to India, a C-46 to Tunisia, seven A-20's to Italy, four C-47's to England and make 70 round trips in C-54's from New York to Europe: Paris, London and Cairo as a charter member of what would become the Military Air Transport command, or more commonly known as M.A.T.S., all because I happened to be at Fort Meade, Maryland when they were looking for volunteers to join the Aviation Cadet Program.

Yes, I was the luckiest "Guinea Pig"or "Pioneer" in the world, both then and now, as I subsequently found that, with faith in the Good Lord, as well as in myself, plus, having such great team workers (and hard work) you can make your own luck and overcome practically any challenge you find in your path.

But special thanks to all those along the line, each of whom provided a necessary link in that chain: from the Pennsylvania National Guard; to the 639th Tank Destroyer Bn.; to the Army Air Corps; to the Pan Am Airways, my fellow "Humpsters"; those the Air Transport command crews (whom I had the pleasure of delivering to their overseas assignments; the thousands of Crescent Caravan passengers, and especially the Good Lord, who helped me gain that self confidence and enabled a young man the back streets of a big city, to tour the four corners of the globe and achieve successful careers in the military, in the business world and in private life.

Andy Kelly
4215 E. 26th. Ave.
Spokane, Wa. 99223

Captain Evans defined.

Everyone has some one who positively influenced his or her life and the one in my case was Captain Harold A. Evans (commanding officer of the 176th Field Artillery Regiment, of the Pennsylvania National Guard's 29th F.A. Division in W.W.II) when we were Federalized) at Fort Meade, Md. in January 1941

Looking back upon my career, in both the military as well as in business after leaving the military, I can read Captain Evan's imprint on almost every area of my life and all for the better. Without him I would not have had much success.

To place this in proper focus I must return to the mid '30's when I lived in a very poor section of Pittsburgh, Pa., but let me digress for a moment. I was a member of a poor family of nine children (of a widowed Mother), six boys and three girls, each of whom was quite blessed with intellect and a sincere desire to gain an education and ultimate success. Their individual school records were quite similar in that each of them was consistently at the top of his or her classes.

Unfortunately, I was a quick learner and seldom needed to study - a habit the rest of the family performed religiously and as their grades so indicated. Being a quick learner I found much time on my hands, especially while in the class room, which resulted in my being the class clown many times.

As a result I became very bored and disinterested in school, so I dropped out of high school after my sophomore year. Fortunately one of my older brothers, a member of the 176th F.A. Batallian (that met one nite each month and spent two weeks each summer on active duty) felt I could use that training.

So brother Jim took me to one of his meetings to try to interest me in joining it. He was one hundred percent right in his thinking as I asked if I could join and they let me sign up. How-ever they had just completed their

1939 summer two week encampment so I had to wait til the next summer and we were sent to Manassas, Virgina to re-enact that famous battle of the civil War, and it was entitled the We reported to a very large open area and were shown how to lay out "tent" city with rows on rows of eight man tents, a latrine as well as a large mess tent where the food was to be prepared. We utilized sleeping bags with eight men to each tent and the immediate areas housed the various batteries and companies separately.

We quickly became familiarized with 45 calibre hand guns, M-1 rifles and even machine guns and later with 75 m.m. and 155 mm howitzers. We had previously been given a detailed account of the original battle of Manassas and were to take the Federal Armies role against other members (as Confederates) of the 29th Division and re-fight the battle.

For the next two weeks we maneuvered against the Rebel Army on practically the same ground the original war was fought. We manned those howitzers as directed by our officers and it was a most interesting, many times confusing, type of battle. But confusing as it was it was very interesting and I couldn't get enough of it.

We reluctantly returned to Pittsburgh after that encampment to impatiently wait until next year. However that was not to be as, due to the war situation in Europe, President Roosevelt was calling many of the National Guard Units to active duty and, as one of them, were Federalized and assigned to Fort Meade, Maryland where we reported into in early January of 1941.

Fort Meade had not had time to build sufficient quarters in that time period so we established tent cities, as we had at Manassas, and moved in while those new barracks were being erected and the new roads being laid in place. The main difficulty was that there was twelve inches of snow on the ground and below freezing temperatures that made it a little uncomfortable sleeping in tents.

As the temperatures began to rise above freezing all of the grounds were turning into mud making it very difficult to march or to train with any of the equipment. One thing was quite noticable, no one was hogging the showers.

Captain Evans was now making his presence known. He said "as we were all members of a year around army that training would proceed just as if it were in mid July. So, though we didn't have sufficient numbers of either 75 m.m. or 155 m.m. howitzers we did have long pieces of pipe mounted on wooden carriages that were mounted upon car wheels and rubber tires.

Regular crews were formed and assigned to those simulated howitzers to train with, despite the mud. Captain Evans said wars and battles are never "called on account of rain". The same held true in marching or simulating firing with machine guns and rifles. The barracks were slowing coming together and we soon moved into ours and they were grand after being in those tents so long. And those army cots looked like hotel beds after those sleeping bags in those cold tents.

Soon there were parade grounds but they meant little to Captain Evans as while the other units used them for drilling, he said we will march at attention every where we would go, even on forced marches across the fields.

As more equipment began to arrive: 45 Calibre pistols for every one, M-1 rifles, new 75 & 155 calibre howitzers, weapons carriers, 6 x 6 troop carriers and trucks to tow the howitzers, jeeps and even motorcycles with side cars. Captain Evans made certain that every member of the battalian must be familiar with every piece of equipment, every fire arm, every vehicle, as some time they may have to operate any of them in emergencies.

We learned to dis-assemble and re-assemble the pistols, rifles and even the machine guns while we were blindfolded so we would not be handicapped in the dark. He made us keep our barracks ultra clean, the cots all made up uniformly the blankets, with square corners and taut enough to bounce quarters off them. The latrines had to be spotless at all times. The footlockers all arranged at the foot of each cot and every piece in them arranged in the exact same order. The extra shoes had to be polished with "spit shines".

Every Friday evening was "clean the barracks night" as every Saturday morning he held "white glove" inspections. He wore white gloves and if they got dirty on anything they touched there were no week end passes.

The area around the barracks were spotless as was the mess hall. Our neighboring units soon began to call us the "Old Ladies' Home" but we soon became the best of the best and always came out tops on any or all inspections by Group Headquarters.

In fact I was on latrine duty one day when a Doctor, a Major from Group headquarters made a surprise inspection and when he had completed it, he said, Private Kelly, you have the cleanest latrine in the entire Division. That later, or so we all had surmised, was the reason for a very special honor I received.

Several months after his inspection, he, the Major, dropped dead of a heart attack. He was given a full course military inspection, casket upon a caisson, an honor guard with rifles, etc and he was laid to rest at the nearby Arlington Cemetery. I was one of the honor guard and never knew why as the only time I had ever met him was when he inspected the latrine. So why I was picked out of a full field artilley division I had no way of knowing. But it was certainly a big, unforgettable honor.

At that time Adolph Hitler's tanks were over running Europe in his Blitz Krieg war and we had no method of combatting them. So evidently some one in Washington, D.C. decided to create a special force that could quickly move in on those tanks, fire special shells that could penetrate that very thick metal they were constructed of, and get out fast.

Now, we had been sent to Fort Meade to become training cadres for all the new "selectees" that was the name given to the draftees. As we were familiar with the large howitzers it was decided to retrain all of us into "Tank Destroyer Battalians" and and be equipped with new "direct fire" 37 m.m. guns that could be attached to the small weapons carrier vehicles, to be quickly hauled into position, set up and fired quickly, then disassembled and rehooked up to those weapons carriers to be quickly moved out again.

Despite Captain Evans constant training in every phase, We had received no increase in rank and when the new tank destroyer units were established we were given "temporary ranks". I was given a platoon of four 37 m.m. guns, actually only mock guns until the new type were manufactured and delivered. I was given six weapons carriers, two "temporary sergeants", four temporary" corporals and eight privates. In the first week I went from PFC (private first class) to temporary corporal, to buck sergeant in a week and to temporary staff sergeant in a month.

Captain Evans assigned two lieutenants to train the battalian of which our platoons were members. They were first lieutenant Phillip Lord and second lieutenant "Rag" Ragland to train us in this new concept. At this time several divisions, to represent the "Blue

Army" who were to go on maneuvers in a territory covering all of both North and South Carolina, against the "Red Army comprised of other Divisions.

Captain Evans had slowly been building our morale, and attitude, to be the best in the entire military in every thing we did. When ever given assignments we were expected to do (and did) those assignments to our very best, better than any other units, and when completed asked "Is that all, Sir, is there anything else required"? That was slowly built into us and we didn't realize then, that we were building pride in ourselves, both individually as well as unit wise.

He expected us to learn every other man's duties, to handle every piece of the equipment, vehicles, fire arms, etc.. To do our best whether it was on K.P., cleaning latrines, marching, guard duty or as clerks. He was a very strict disciplinarian in all phase of our training - but - there was nothing he ordered us to do that he couldn't do better and did so many times.

It wasn't til later, when I was in the Army Air Corps Celestial Navigation school at the University of Miami, and found those Cadet Schools had very strict discipline in every area and many cadets picked up (almost daily) demerits for some sort of infraction, be it in attitude, in dress code, class rooms, for which they had to "walk tours" on the week ends.

I never picked up a single demerit in cadet school because of the strict training, the self confidence, the self pride that Captain Evans had built into us. We all learned that to do our utmost in carrying out any assignment, to do it better than anyone else and then ask if we could do more.

That applied to both the military and civilian life and I told my sons, when they were in the service to follow that principle. Later when my grandson's, who while in the military, would call or write me with problems I would tell them to use that principle also and they did, quite successfully.

As I said, Captain Evans was a man ahead of his time which was really emphacised to me when my youngest son joined the Navy and was a sonar operator on submarines. He told me the Navy policy aboard submarines was that no man was accepted as a permanent crew member until he had read thirty manuals pertaining to duty aboard that vessel.

They would read a chapter and have a petty officer initial at the end of each chapter that he had done so. Whenever the complete manual was finished, it would be initialed by an Ensign it had been accomplished. It wasn't until every chapter and every manual were completely read and signed that that particular crewman was accepted.

What they had accomplished in those thirty manuals was to learn every other crewman's duty and be ready to assume it, when and if necessary. This was exactly what Captain Evans had done with us. We, too, knew every other man's duty if that need ever arose. That is why the submarine crews were so highly acclaimed and if one ever had occasion to leave that duty he would be quickly snapped up by the surface fleet, as they were the best trained in the entire Navy. (Captain Evans was years ahead of his time in the military)

Andy Kelly, Colonel U.S.A.F retired
4215 E. 26th Av.
Spokane, Wa. 99223
(509 532 8250)

Shot Down Zero With 45 Pistol?

• The strangest tale of WW II happened in 1943, the year I was flying "The Hump." I was a member of the Army Air Corps Ferry Command (later to be the Air Transport Command) stationed at Chabua, in the Province of Assam. We were the source of all material to be used in the area between eastern part of India, Burma and western China (Kunming and Chungking) and the 10th and 14th Air Forces stationed in our theatre.

The 10th A.F.'s Seventh Bomb Group's Ninth Bomb squadron, on March 31, 1943, was dispatched to destroy a railroad bridge at Pyinmana (Burma) between Rangoon and Mandalay.

The formation, of B-24's, was led by Col. Conrad Necrason, the Seventh Bomb group's commander. The B-24 on his right wing was piloted by 1/Lt. Lloyd Jenkins and his co-pilot was 2/Lt. Owen Baggett – who was about to earn a distinction never before (or since) achieved in Air Force history. "He shot down a Japanese Zero with his side arm – a 45 mm pistol!"

When Lloyd's B-24 was so severely attacked, the entire crew had to bail out – and as they were floating earthward the Jap Zero's began to strafe the helpless airmen in those chutes.

Lt. Baggett tried to de-

Most amazing feat of W.W.11 - Japanese Zero shot down with 45 calibre side arm by pilot in a parachute !

ceive the Jap's by becoming limp and pretending to be dead, but he kept his 45 concealed in his left hand and when the Jap pilot slowed and opened his canopy for a closer look, Lt. Baggett put four shots into the plane, one of which hit the pilot causing the plane to stall out and crash.

Baggett and several other survivors were imprisoned by the Japanese. Later on, Col. Harry Melton (C.O. of the 311th Fighter Group) was shot down, captured and passed on through the same prison camp.

Col. Melton told Baggett that a Japanese colonel had told him of a bizarre incident in which a Zero was found crashed but the pilot was thrown clear. Upon investigation of the pilot's wounds he found to have only a single shot to the head – but it was from a hand

gun, not from aircraft armament.

Col. Melton knew the plane was found in area where Baggett had been shot down and was going to make an official report of his finding after his release from the prison camp. However, he lost his life while still a prisoner of war.

Baggett eventually was released and resumed his career in the Air Force and retired as a Colonel. When the incident was later reported, there was no reasonable doubt that Lt. Baggett had performed a most unique feat of valor that was never before, or since, duplicated, a once in a millenium act, he had shot down an enemy fighter aircraft with his hand gun while suspended from a parachute. ANDY KELLY.

Andrew Kelly

About the Author

Retired military officer (command & staff level)

Retired H.V.A.C. Specialist

Retired Manufacturer's Rep. (plumbing & heating Ind.)

Past chairman board of trustees at a major university

Past director of a municipal park board

Past director Fairchild AFB retiree activities office

Present state director American-Ireland Political Ed. Comm.

Presently freelance writer plumbing & heating products:

    Specifying products

    Installation procedures

    Troubleshooting & servicing hydronic heating systems

Presently freelance writer:

    Military personnel of WWII

    C.B.I. Theatre (Hump)

    Ferrying WWII aircraft:

Ferry Command
Air Transport Command
Military airline origins:
Crescent Caravan
Military Air Transport Service
Air Corps Celestial Navigation
Veteran of all military theatres in WWII: The C.B.I., North Africa, Mid-East, India, China, European Theatre, etc. Have over 70 round trips from New York to England.

Printed in the United States
955100004B

9 781403 321084